Trinity Footprints

Roger Skrenes

⊕*ENROUTE*
Make the time

En Route Books and Media, LLC
5705 Rhodes Avenue
St. Louis, MO 63109

Cover credit: TJ Burdick

Library of Congress Control Number: 2019939038

Copyright © 2019
Roger Skrenes
All rights reserved.

ISBN-13: 978-1-950108-04-6
ISBN-10: 1-950108-04-X

Table of Contents

Introduction

Before the coming of Christ, men and women around the world worshipped many gods and goddesses. They transformed many natural mysteries of life into a god or goddess and then invented imaginative stories to explain their significance. (*2 Peter 1:16*) The truth is that God was in many ways unknown before the coming of Jesus.

No one has ever seen God;
the only begotten God (the Son, Jesus)
being in the bosom of (God)
the Father, that one declared him.
John 1:18

When Jesus walked among us on this planet, he revealed to us something of the interior life of God. We learned, for example, that there are three co-eternal subjects in the one God. This 3-in-1 structure is fundamental to our world because God is the author of the universe. God (the father) . . . in these last days spoke to us in a Son (Jesus), whom he appointed heir of all things; through whom he made the ages . . .

Hebrews 1:1-2

God said: "Let Us make
man in Our image,
according to Our likeness."

Genesis 1:26

This book asserts there are evidences of the "tri-une" nature of God in both people and in the world. However, such instances of God's presence are not generally known by Christians or by others around the world. This book is an attempt to inform readers of these triune (or three-in-one) footprints of God in everyday life. By reading this book the reader should better perceive the presence of the triune God in our world and see how God impacts our life in mysterious ways."

Roger Skrenes

The invisible things of Him
are clearly seen from
the creation of the world,
being understood by the things
(He has) made ...

Romans 1:20

— Roger Skrenes

I. Creation:
Space, Time & Matter

Creation

Creation precedes evolution. Creation refers to God's calling matter into existence from nothing. Each of the three subjects in God is involved in this work.

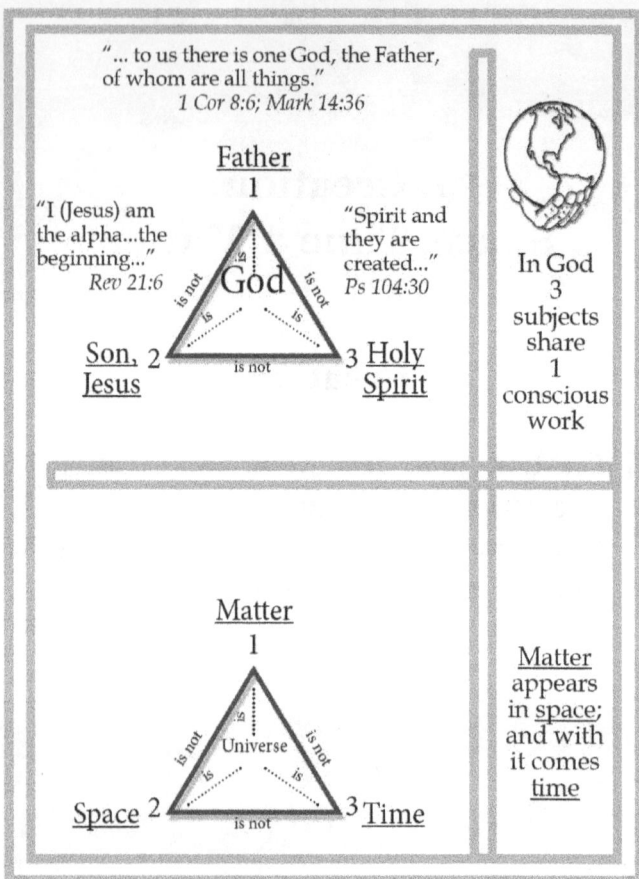

"... to us there is one God, the Father, of whom are all things."
1 Cor 8:6; Mark 14:36

Father
1

"I (Jesus) am the alpha...the beginning..."
Rev 21:6

is not   is   is not

God

"Spirit and they are created..."
Ps 104:30

In God
3
subjects
share
1
conscious
work

Son, 2 Jesus   is not   3 Holy Spirit

Matter
1

is not   is   is not

Universe

Space 2   is not   3 Time

Matter
appears
in space;
and with
it comes
time

The language of the OT is Hebrew. There are two words meaning "creation" in the Hebrew language. One of these words is "Bara," meaning to create something out of nothing. "Bara" is used fifty times in the OT when speaking of God. (See: *Genesis 1:1*)

Creation is a direct work of God. Evolution is an indirect work of God. Creation is that point where God brings matter into existence from nothing. Evolution is what happens to matter after it is created. In evolution, God has worked through secondary causes. He uses "laws" in matter, some of which are known to science.

> By faith we understand the ages
> to have been adjusted by
> the Word of God
> so that things unseen have
> become by things appearing.
> *Hebrews 11:3*

Space

"God... in the height of Heaven?"
Job 22: 12

Father
1

is

is not   God   is not

is   is

Son, 2   is not   3 **Holy**
Jesus   **Spirit**
▲

"Wide is the... way   "Spirit searches...
(away from God)"   the deep things..."
Matt 7:13   *1 Cor 2:10*

In God
3
subjects
share
1
Presence

Height
1

is

is not   Space   is not

is   is

Width 2   is not   3 **Depth**

In space
3
dimensions
describe
1
volume

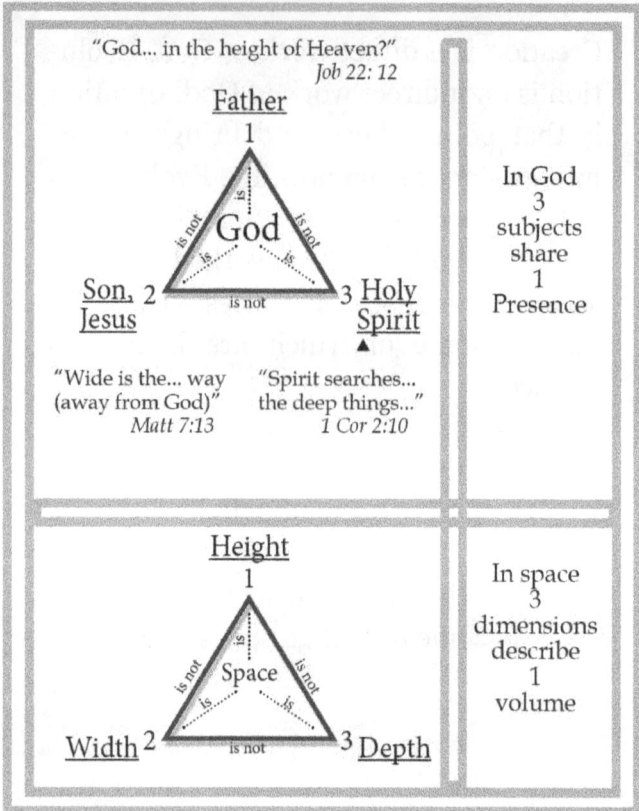

God made the universe. The shape of each thing in it is described by three measurements: height, width and depth. We humans "see" in three dimensions (3-

8

D). This outer three-ness of all things is a mirror of God's inner three-ness.

Time

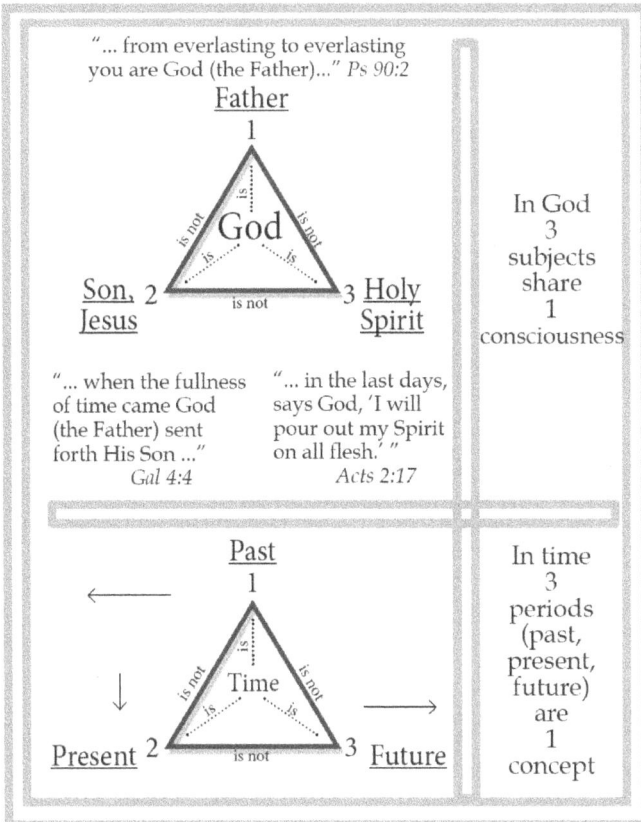

"... from everlasting to everlasting you are God (the Father)..." *Ps 90:2*

Father
1

is
is not
is not
is
is

God

Son, 2
Jesus

is not

3 Holy
Spirit

In God
3
subjects
share
1
consciousness

"... when the fullness of time came God (the Father) sent forth His Son ..." *Gal 4:4*

"... in the last days, says God, 'I will pour out my Spirit on all flesh.' " *Acts 2:17*

Past
1

is
is not
is not
is
is

Time

Present 2

is not

3 Future

In time
3
periods
(past, present, future)
are
1
concept

9

God is eternal. He existed before time. Time came into being when God created the universe.

The three subjects in God (Father, Son and Holy Spirit) are co-eternal. There never was a time when the Son was not the Son. The Son or Word is, in essence, one with the Father:

> The Father is in me
> and I (Jesus, the Word)
> am in the Father.
>
> *John 14:10*

> Yahweh (the Father)
> possessed me (Jesus)
> in the beginning of his ways...
> From everlasting I was there,
> from the beginning...
>
> *Proverbs 8:23*

Hydrogen Atoms

Hydrogen atoms make up nine of every ten atoms in the universe. The heavier atoms were created in part by combining the lighter hydrogen atoms.

"In the beginning God (the Father) created ..."
Gen 1:1;
1 Cor 8:6

Father
1

is
God
is not | is not
is ... is
is not

Son, 2 ─────────────── 3 Holy
Jesus | Spirit

"... by him (Christ) all things were created."
Col 1:16

"Your Spirit ... created"
Ps 104:30

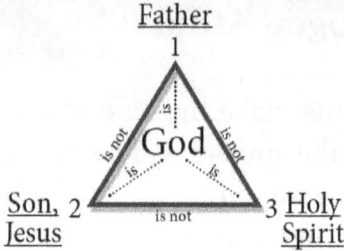

In God
3
subjects
share
1
Power

One Proton
Positive (+) charge
1

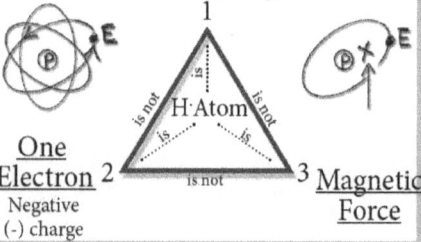

is
H·Atom
is not | is not
is ... is
is not

One
Electron 2 ─────────────── 3 Magnetic
Force

Negative
(-) charge

In
Hydrogen
3
parts
make-up
1
atom

12

Hydrogen Atoms	Subjects in God
Proton (+)	Father unbegotten
makes up most	
of atom's weight	
Electron (-)	
a) orbits proton	
b) makes the	Son/Jesus
"chemistry"	a) "One with
of an atom	Father"
	John14:9
Magnetic Force	b) makes Father's
mysteriously	voice heard
holds proton (1)	Holy Spirit
and electron (2)	mysterious love
together.	between Father
	and Son

Atoms

The universe is made of 92 basic atoms. Each of these atoms exists in three ways: as a solid, as a liquid, or as a gas. This three-ness is rooted in God, who made the universe in his own image.

Roger Skrenes

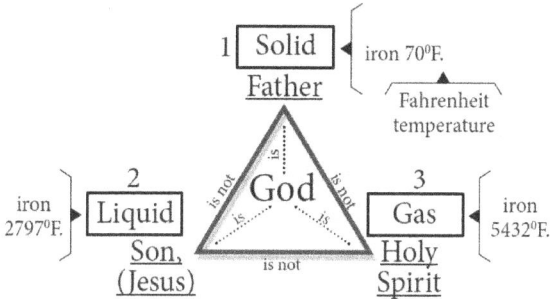

	Atoms & number		'Farenheit Temps ^{0}		
			Solid $\longrightarrow$ Liquid $\longrightarrow$ Gas		
1	Hydrogen	in stars	-440^{0}F	-435^{0}F	-413^{0}F
2	Helium	balloons	-460	-458	-452
6	Carbon	diamond	70	6422	7120
8	Oxygen	in air	-365	-361	-297
13	Aluminum	planes	70^{0}F	1220	4473
14	Silicon	glass		2570	4271
20	Calcium	in bones		1548	2709
26	Iron	in steel		2797	5432
29	Copper	wire	room temp	787	1665
47	Silver	in film		1762	4014
79	Gold	jewelry		1945	5371
80	Mercury	switches	-40	-38	675

The three-ness of the universe is rooted in God. This is because in God there are three subjects: Father, Son and Holy Spirit.

Atoms have only three states or ways of

being: not two, four, five or any other number. These three states of every atom are viewed as an image of God.

Electrons

Electron particles fly around
the center of each atom.

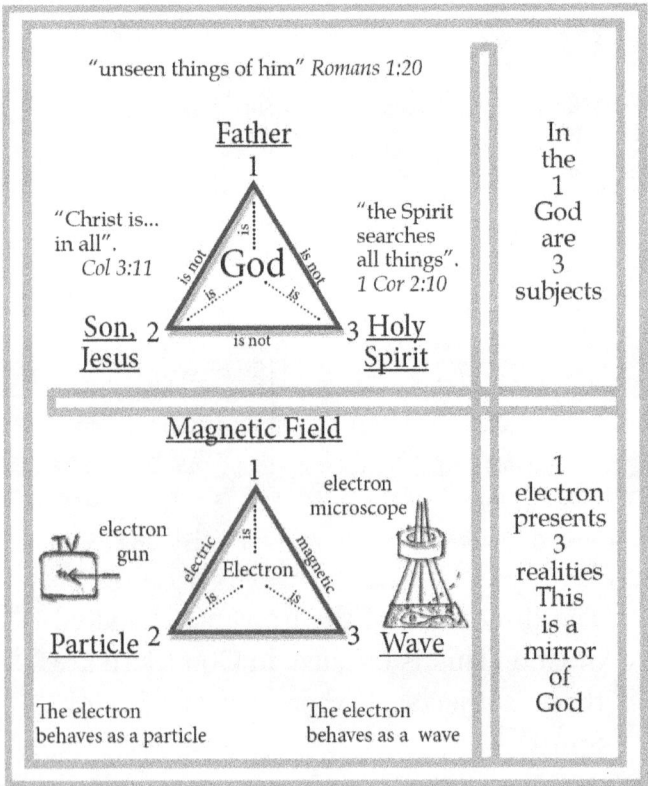

"unseen things of him" *Romans 1:20*

Father
1

"Christ is... in all".
Col 3:11

is not

is

God

is not

"the Spirit searches all things".
1 Cor 2:10

Son, 2
Jesus

is not

3 Holy
Spirit

In
the
1
God
are
3
subjects

Magnetic Field
1

electric

electron
microscope

is

Electron

magnetic

electron
gun

TV

is

is

Particle 2

3 Wave

1
electron
presents
3
realities
This
is a
mirror
of
God

The electron
behaves as a particle

The electron
behaves as a wave

All atoms in the universe have electrons. All electrons have particle, wave and field effects—3-in-1. These 3-in-1 effects can be seen as a mirror of their Creator.

Stars

Our star is called the "sun." The sun gives the earth radiation, light and heat. Plants use sunlight to make food (sugar) and oxygen for animals to breathe.

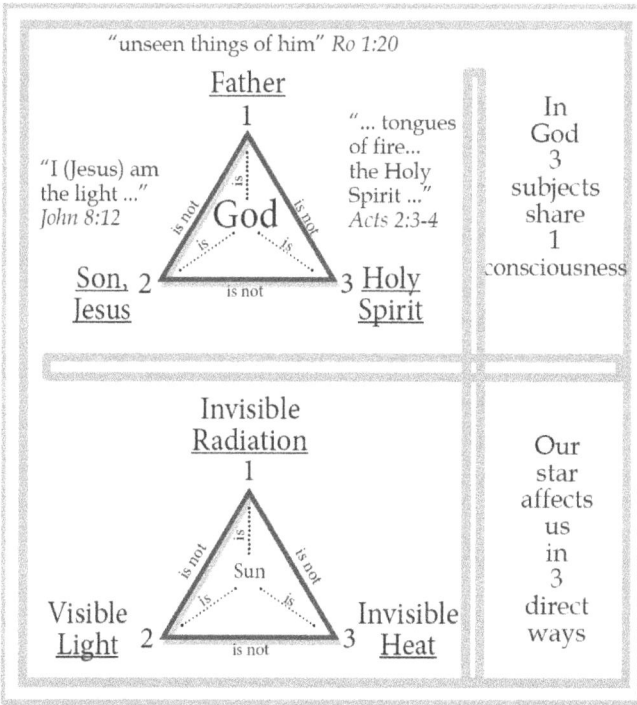

"unseen things of him" *Ro 1:20*

Father
1

"... tongues of fire... the Holy Spirit ..."
Acts 2:3-4

"I (Jesus) am the light ..."
John 8:12

God

is
is not
is not
is

Son, 2
Jesus
is not
3 Holy
Spirit

In God 3 subjects share 1 consciousness

Invisible
Radiation
1

is
is not
is not
is

Sun

Visible
Light 2
is not
3 Invisible
Heat

Our star affects us in 3 direct ways

--->

$$6\ H_2O + 6\ CO_2 + sunlight = C6H_{12}O_6 + 6\ O_2$$

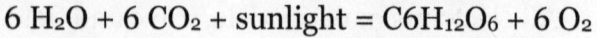

water + carbon
dioxide

sugar + oxygen
(the body's fuel)

Light is very important for
the production of food on earth.

A chain of sugar molecules
makes up one starch molecule.
Starch molecules are the basis of bread.

Primary Colors

White-light consists of a
mixture of three
primary colors: red,
green and blue. All
other known colors are
made by combining
these three.

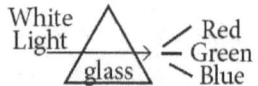

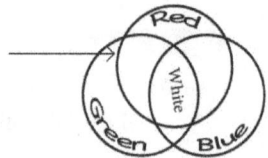

"... gift is from above coming down from the Father of lights." *James 1:17*

Father

"Jesus said: 'I am the light of the world' " *John 8:12*

1

God

is   *is not*

is not   *is*

is not

Son, 2   3 Holy
Jesus   Spirit

"... in your light (God), we see light." *Pss 36:9*

In God are 3 subjects

Red Light

1

Light

is   *is not*

is not   *is*

is not

Green 2   3 Blue
Light   Light

In white light are 3 primary colors

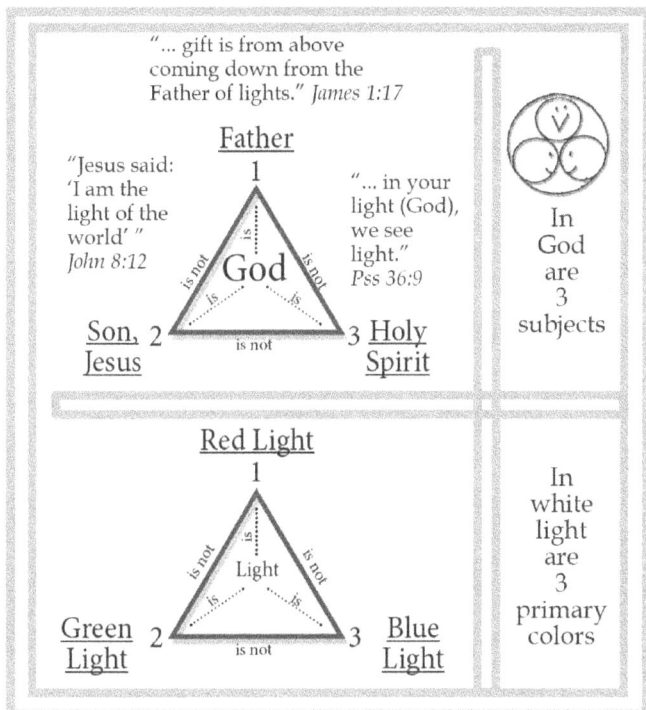

Color motion pictures and color television use the 3-in-1 system to create all color combinations on the screen. This cannot be accidental in a universe that owes its existence to the Triune God.

Just as red, green, and blue are white light, so also the Father, Son and Holy Spirit are one God.

19

Fire

"God (the Father) is a consuming fire ..."
Deut 4:24; Heb 12:29

Father
1

"I (Jesus) came to cast fire on the earth ..."
Luke 12:49

is not   is   is not

God

"Baptize you in the Holy Spirit and fire."
Matt 3:11

is   is

is not

Son, Jesus 2   3 **Holy Spirit**

In God
1
fire
is shared
by
3
subjects

"God called to Moses from the burning bush..."
Exodus 3:2-4

noise
light   heat

"His (Jesus) eyes were like a flame of <u>fire</u>
Rev 1:14

Noise
1

is not   is   is not

Combustion

"... tongues as of <u>fire</u> the Holy Spirit..."
Acts 2:3

is   is

is not

2 **Light**   3 **Heat**

Fire
creates
3
effects
(noise,
light
and heat)

Fire occurs when something burns.

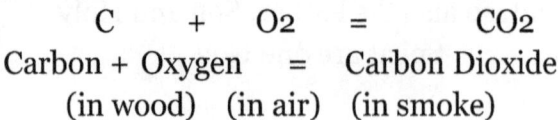

$$C \quad + \quad O_2 \quad = \quad CO_2$$

Carbon + Oxygen = Carbon Dioxide
(in wood)   (in air)   (in smoke)

Fire is especially important as
a source of heat in winter for humans.

Water

About three-fourths of the earth is
covered by water. Our body is also three-
fourths water. Water, like its creator,
reveals itself in three ways.

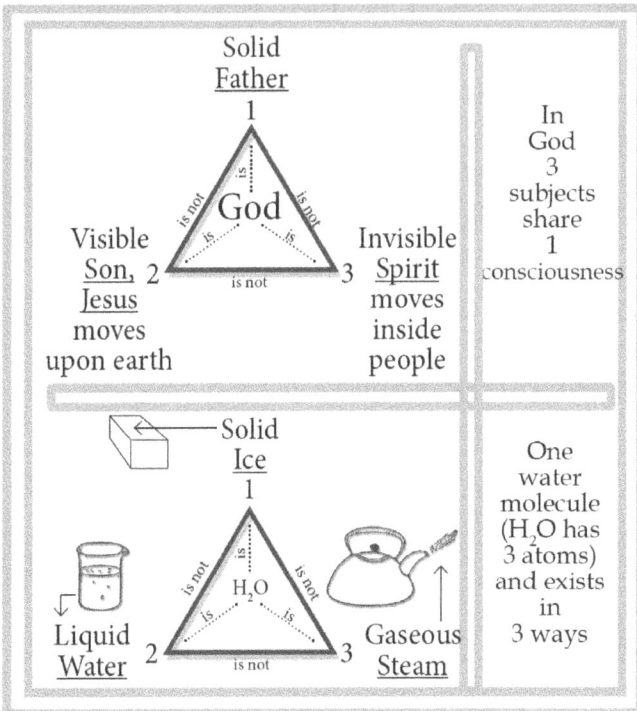

Solid
Father
1

is
is not   is not

God

Visible   is   is   Invisible
Son, 2 _____ 3 Spirit
Jesus   is not   moves
moves   inside
upon earth   people

In
God
3
subjects
share
1
consciousness

Solid
Ice
1

is
is not   is not

H₂O

Liquid   is   is   Gaseous
Water 2 _____ 3 Steam
            is not

One
water
molecule
(H₂O has
3 atoms)
and exists
in
3 ways

Ice (Father)
By the breath of God ice is given.

Job 37:10

He casts forth ice, like morsels.

Ps 147:17

Water (Son)
The rock (source of water on the
Exodus) was Christ.

Exod 17, 6; 1 Cor 10:4

Jesus came ... walking on water.

Matt 14:25

Jesus said ... (then) water became wine.
John 2:7-9 ... living water (Jesus).

John 4:10

Steam (Holy Spirit)
A mist went up from the earth.

Gen 2:6

He makes vapors rise."

Jer 10:13

II. Life

Plants

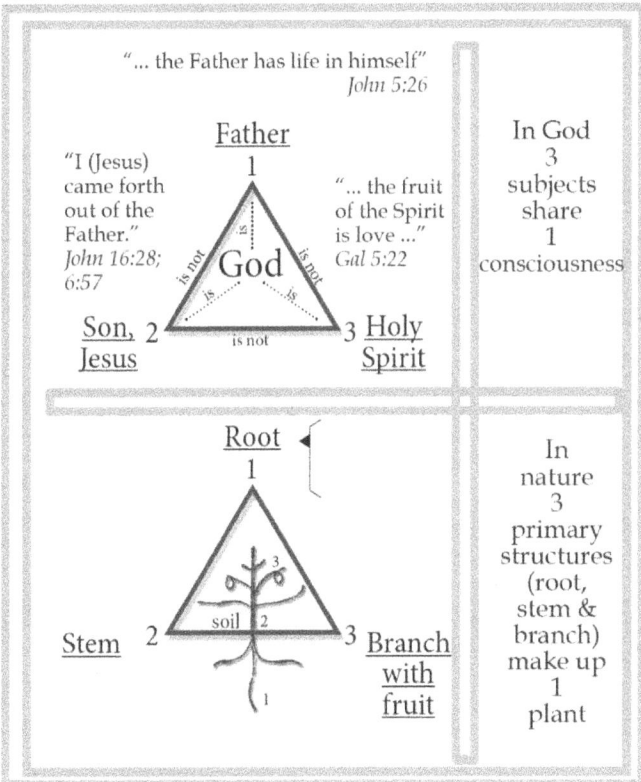

"... the Father has life in himself"
John 5:26

Father
1

"I (Jesus) came forth out of the Father."
John 16:28; 6:57

"... the fruit of the Spirit is love ..."
Gal 5:22

God

is
is not
is not
is not

Son, Jesus 2

3 Holy Spirit

In God
3
subjects
share
1
consciousness

Root
1

Stem 2

soil 2

3 Branch with fruit

In nature
3
primary
structures
(root,
stem &
branch)
make up
1
plant

Plant Structure

1. A stem is connected to a *root*.
    Jesus is "in the Father ..."

    John 14:10

2. A branch comes forth from a stem.
   The Spirit comes forth from Jesus.

   John 15:26

3. Fruit comes forth from branches. Love,
   peace, and joy are fruits of the Spirit.

   Gal 5:22

Animals

"Father gave you being, made
you and by whom you subsist?"
Deut 32:6

"(Jesus)
the author
of life ..."
Acts 3:15

"In him
(Jesus)
was life ..."
John 1:4

<u>Father</u>
1

is

is not

is not

God

is

is

<u>Son,</u> 2
<u>Jesus</u>

is not

3 <u>Holy</u>
<u>Spirit</u>

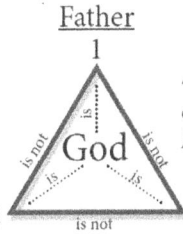

"... the Spirit
of truth"
John 16:13

In God
3
subjects
share
1
consciousness

<u>Being</u>
<u>matter</u>
1

is

is not

is not

Creature

is

is

2
<u>Life</u>

is not

3
<u>Intelligence</u>

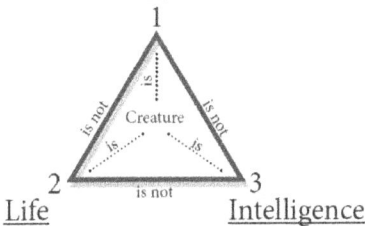

In
1
creature
are
3
levels
of
existence

Creatures are a composite of matter, its proper organization into life, and eventual blossoming into intelligence.

This process began with the formation of our galaxy about 13.7 billion years ago. It continued with the birth of our star the sun, and our planet the earth about 4.6 billion years ago; and then issued forth into signs of life about 1 billion years ago.

Creatures with intelligence began about 600 million years ago. Fish appeared about 500 million years ago.

Amphibians about 400 million. Reptiles about 300 million. Mammals about 200. Primates about 60 million. Apes about 10 million. And humans about 2 million.

All of these episodes in God's work are found within each human person.

My Creation

"God created man in his own image ..."

Genesis 1:27

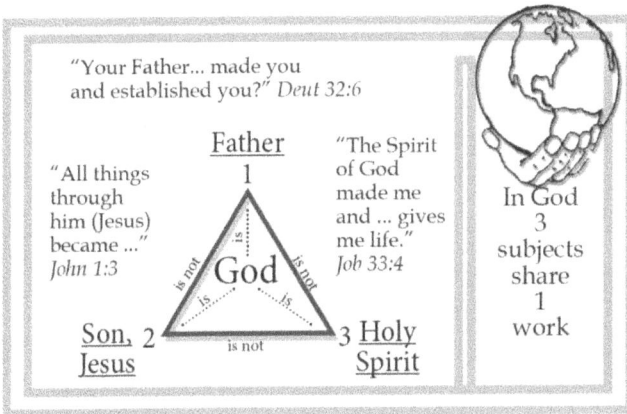

"Your Father... made you and established you?" *Deut 32:6*

Father
1

"All things through him (Jesus) became ..."
John 1:3

"The Spirit of God made me and ... gives me life."
Job 33:4

God
is — is not — is — is not — is not

Son, 2
Jesus

3 Holy
Spirit

In God
3
subjects
share
1
work

Jesus and the Father are One in Being (God), but they are not one subject.

... believe the works (miracles I do)
that you may know that
the Father is in Me and
I am in the Father.

John 10:38

Sight

One "sight"-ing involves three parts:
the *object* seen, the *image* in the eye,
and
the *intellect* that connects them
together.

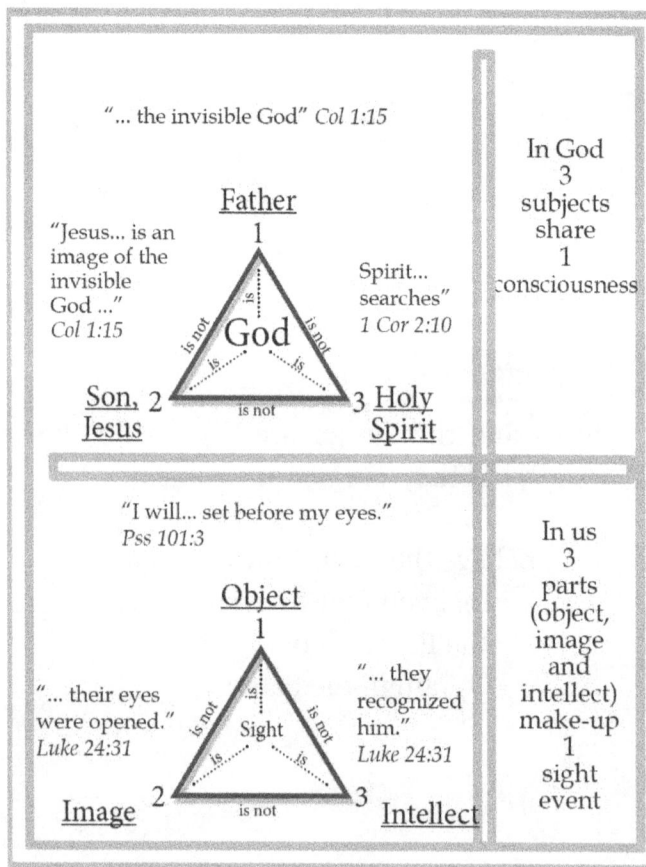

"... the invisible God" *Col 1:15*

Father
1

"Jesus... is an image of the invisible God ..." *Col 1:15*

Spirit... searches" *1 Cor 2:10*

is not · is · God · is · is not

Son, 2 Jesus   is not   3 Holy Spirit

In God
3
subjects
share
1
consciousness

"I will... set before my eyes." *Pss 101:3*

Object
1

"... their eyes were opened." *Luke 24:31*

"... they recognized him." *Luke 24:31*

is not · is · Sight · is · is not

Image 2   is not   3 Intellect

In us
3
parts
(object,
image
and
intellect)
make-up
1
sight
event

The Trinity is evident in the first lines of the Bible. In its words are included the three subjects of the one God: Father, Spirit, and Word.

Gen 1:1
"In the beginning God (the Father) created the heavens and the earth."

Gen 1:2
"And the Spirit of God moved gently over the face of the waters."

Gen 1:3
"Then God said [with His Word]: 'Let light be,' and there was light."

Hearing

Hearing involves three parts:

The sound-*source*,
the *ear* as an instrument,
and
the *intellect* as its interpreter.

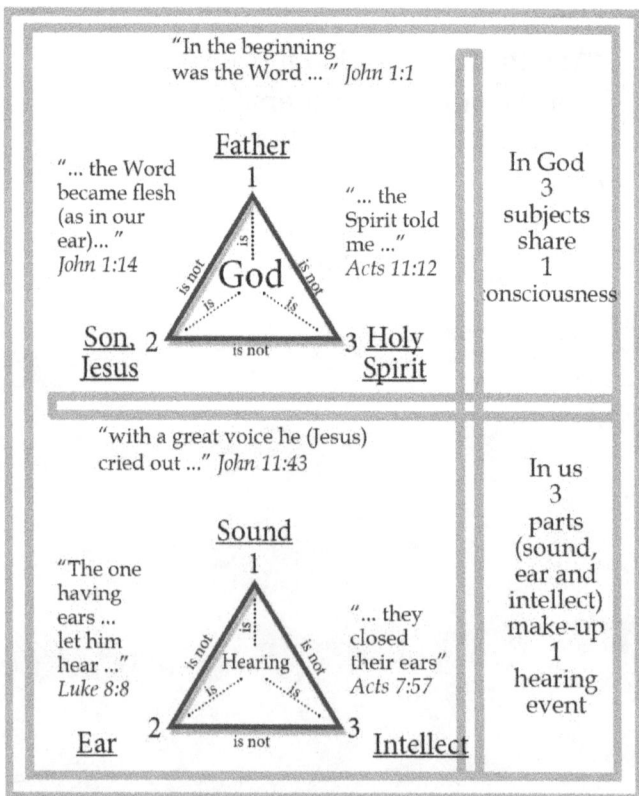

"In the beginning
was the Word ..." *John 1:1*

Father
1

"... the Word
became flesh
(as in our
ear)..."
John 1:14

"... the
Spirit told
me ..."
Acts 11:12

is not · is · is not

God

is · is not · is

Son, 2
Jesus

is not

3 Holy
Spirit

In God
3
subjects
share
1
consciousness

"with a great voice he (Jesus)
cried out ..." *John 11:43*

Sound
1

"The one
having
ears ...
let him
hear ..."
Luke 8:8

"... they
closed
their ears"
Acts 7:57

is · is not

Hearing

is · is not · is

Ear
2

is not

3
Intellect

In us
3
parts
(sound,
ear and
intellect)
make-up
1
hearing
event

Sound, like God, is invisible (not seen). Yet both are ever-present in our world. The ear makes us aware of sound. Jesus makes us aware of God. (*John 1:18*)

Hands

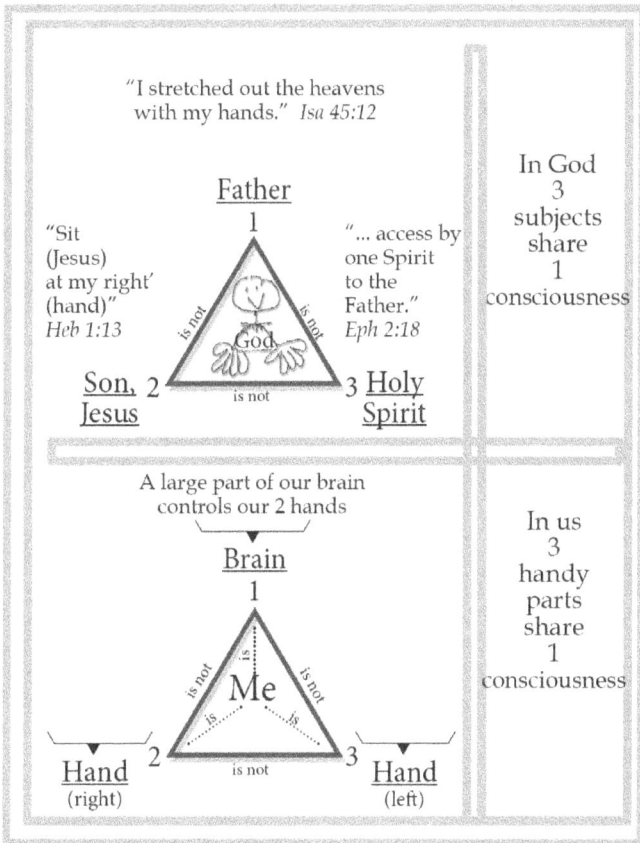

"I stretched out the heavens with my hands." *Isa 45:12*

In God
3 subjects
share
1 consciousness

Father
1

"Sit (Jesus) at my right' (hand)" *Heb 1:13*

"... access by one Spirit to the Father." *Eph 2:18*

is not   God   is not

Son, 2 ————— is not ————— 3 Holy
Jesus   Spirit

A large part of our brain controls our 2 hands

Brain
1

In us
3 handy parts share
1 consciousness

is not   Me   is not

is   is

Hand 2 ————— is not ————— 3 Hand
(right)   (left)

This model of the Trinity shows God the Father with two hands: Jesus as his right hand and the Holy Spirit as his left hand.

This model was conceived of by Saint Irenaeus, Bishop of Lyons, France in about 180 AD. In recent times it has been discovered that a large portion of our higher brain (cerebral cortex) directs hand-operations.

Reproduction

Each birth is a triad: father, mother, and baby. The 3 are 1 family.

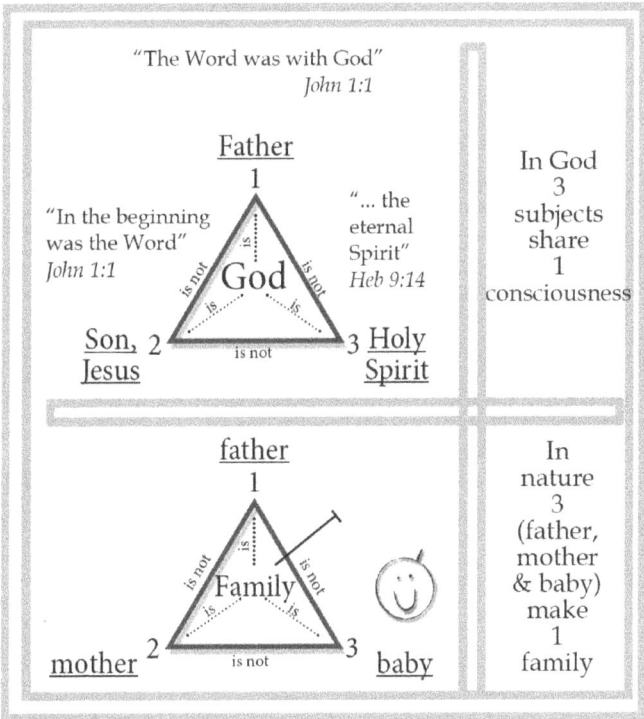

"The Word was with God"
John 1:1

Father
1

"In the beginning
was the Word"
John 1:1

"... the
eternal
Spirit"
Heb 9:14

God

is not   is
is   is not
is not

Son,
Jesus
2

3 Holy
Spirit

In God
3
subjects
share
1
consciousness

father
1

Family

is not   is
is   is not
is not

mother
2

3
baby

In
nature
3
(father,
mother
& baby)
make
1
family

In God there is no reproduction.
God has always existed. God is eternal.

In the beginning was the Word
(Son, Jesus) and the Word was
with God (the Father) ...

John 1:1

Father ... you loved me (Jesus)
before the foundation of the world.

John 17:24

The Holy Spirit proceeds from
the Father and the Son.
He also is eternal:
"... the eternal Spirit."

Hebrews 9:14

Roger Skrenes

Clones

Clones are identical life-forms.
"Identical twins" are clones.
Clones look identical because they have
identical genes: the same DNA.

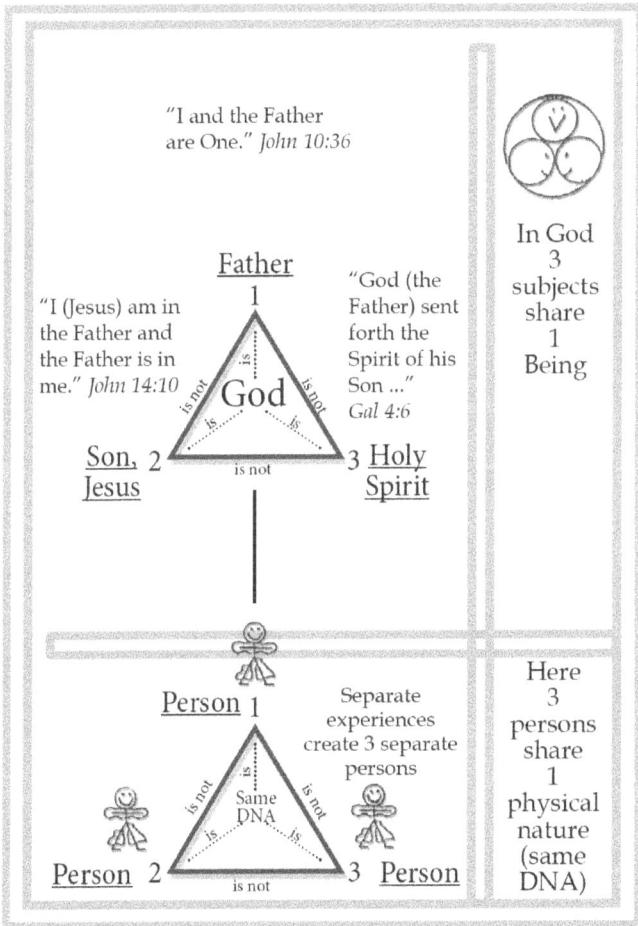

Twins are natural-born clones. They are remarkably alike. Yet, as they grow, they experience different relations among both family and friends, with different results. Each becomes his own person while remaining genetically identical.

In God each subject is identical in all ways except by "relations." The Father begets. The Son (Word of the Father) is begotten. The Holy Spirit proceeds from the love between the Father and the Son. Therefore, while all three are one God, each is by relations his own subject.

On earth each person, even identical twins, have their own consciousness. However, in God three subjects share one consciousness.

III. The Human Mind

Life

Our one life consists of three key areas:

1) *Being*, or our existence (genetic start)
2) *Knowledge*, or internalizing the world
3) *Love*, or choosing among possible goods

Trinity Footprints

"... the Father has <u>life</u> in Himself" *John 5:26*

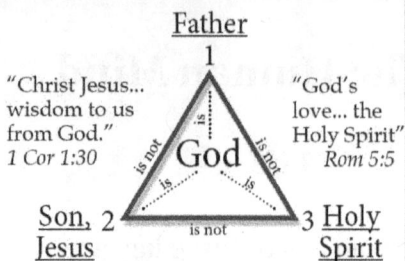

<u>Father</u>
1

"Christ Jesus... wisdom to us from God." *1 Cor 1:30*

"God's love... the Holy Spirit" *Rom 5:5*

is not · is · is not

God

is · is

<u>Son,</u> 2
<u>Jesus</u>

is not

3 <u>Holy</u>
<u>Spirit</u>

In God
3
subjects
share
1
consciousness

Being is the "essence" of a thing. The more we know, the greater is our being.

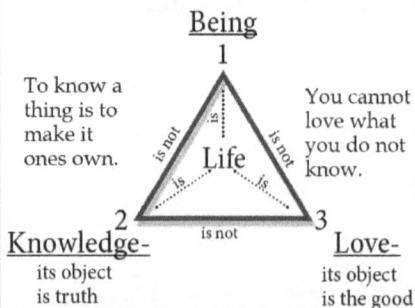

<u>Being</u>
1

To know a thing is to make it ones own.

You cannot love what you do not know.

is not · is · is not

Life

is · is

2
<u>Knowledge-</u>
its object
is truth

is not

3
<u>Love-</u>
its object
is the good

In us
3
areas
(being,
knowledge
and love)
make up
1
consciousness

The world exhibits order:

1) All creation has being.
2) Plants have the beginnings of life.
3) Lower animals have sensory knowledge. They see, hear, and know objects outside themselves.
4) Apes and monkeys have the beginnings of *reason*.
5) Human beings have complex reasoning and knowledge of love.

Consciousness

To be "conscious" we need past
and present experience.
No past — we are lost.
No present — we are "unconscious."

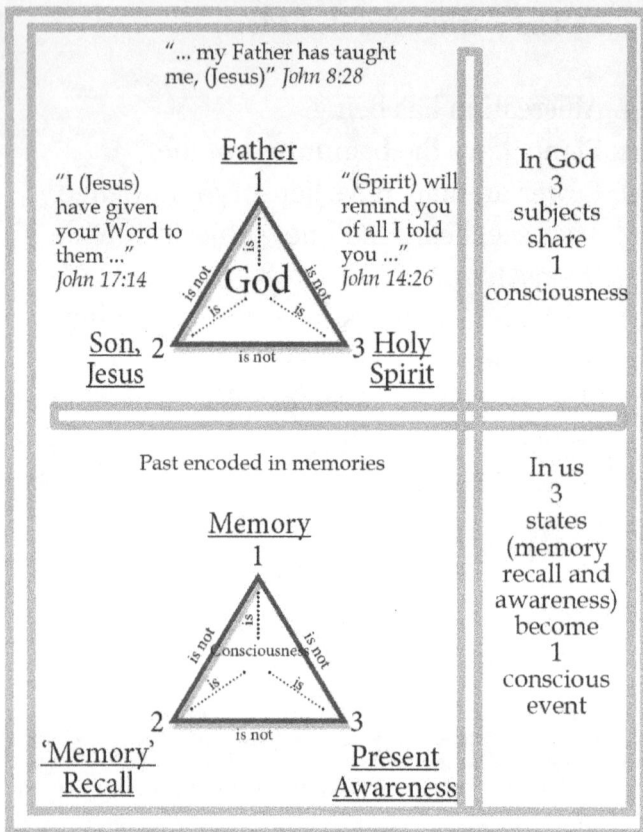

"... my Father has taught me, (Jesus)" *John 8:28*

Father
1

"I (Jesus) have given your Word to them ..." *John 17:14*

"(Spirit) will remind you of all I told you ..." *John 14:26*

is not
God
is not
is
is
is not

Son, 2
Jesus

3 Holy
Spirit

In God
3
subjects
share
1
consciousness

Past encoded in memories

Memory
1

is not
Consciousness
is not
is
is
is not

2
'Memory'
Recall

3
Present
Awareness

In us
3
states
(memory
recall and
awareness)
become
1
conscious
event

A key factor in the notion of
consciousness is memory storage.
The greater the number of
memories stored, the greater
the level of consciousness.

			Memory Storage
	800M	1-celled animals	Very small (no brain)
	500M	Fish (scales)	Some
M = millions of years ago	300M	Reptiles (scales)	More
	200M	Mammals (hair)	Good
	10M	Apes (hair)	Better
	2M	People	Best

Mind

Our one mind has three essential components:

1) Memory: stored knowledge

2) Intellect: possessing "forms" of things without their matter

3) Will: instrument for choosing good or evil

"God ... his understanding is infinite." *Ps 147:5*

Father
1

"... all things are naked and laid open to His (Jesus) eyes." *Heb 4:13*

"God operates all things according to ... his will." *Eph 1:11*

God

is · is not · is not · is · is · is not

Son, Jesus 2

3 Holy Spirit

In God 3 subjects share 1 consciousness

Stored sense data, and reasoned judgements

Memory
(storage)
1

Presents goods to the will from which to choose: Input

Choosing to do, or not to do something: Output

Mind

is · is not · is not · is · is · is not

Intellect 2 (reason)

3 Will (choice)

In us 3 faculties (memory, intellect and will) create 1 consciousness

---

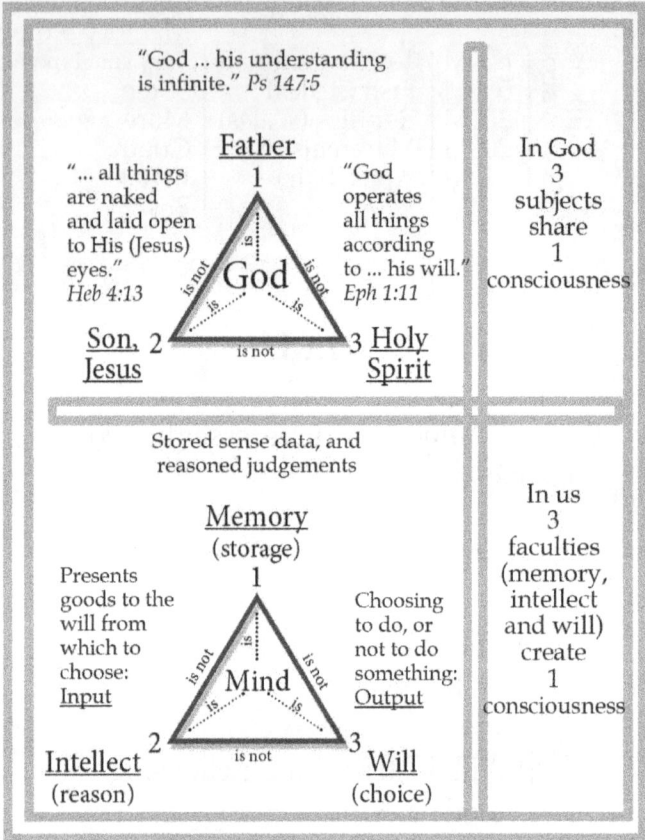

There are two essential operations within God:

(1) knowing and (2) willing

Processions within God are just two:

1) Word, from His intellect (= Son of God)
2) Love, from His Will (= Holy Spirit)

These two processions in God are also eternal. They had no beginning in time.

Only that which is *within* God can possess the divine essence. Creation is outside of God, and therefore is not God. Pantheism is excluded.

Intellect
(Reason)

"The eyes of the Lord are in every place..."
Prov 15:3; Heb 4:13

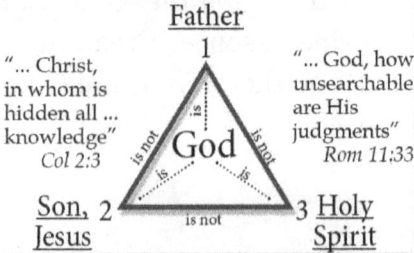

Father
1

"... Christ, in whom is hidden all ... knowledge"
Col 2:3

"... God, how unsearchable are His judgments"
Rom 11:33

God

is
is not
is
is
is not

Son, 2   3 Holy
Jesus   Spirit

is not

In God
3
subjects
share
1
consciousness

Grasping qualties of things:
seeing, hearing, feeling, tasting, etc.

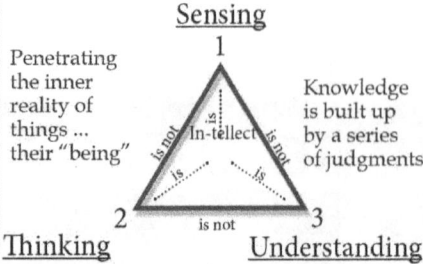

Sensing
1

Penetrating the inner reality of things ... their "being"

Knowledge is built up by a series of judgments

In-tellect

is
is not
is
is
is not

2   3
is not

Thinking   Understanding

Our
1
intellect
has
3
roles
(sensing,
thinking
and
judgment)

Our one intellect has three roles:

(1) Sensing, or acquiring "forms" or perceptions of things
(2) Knowing, or "thinking" with object forms, manipulated free from matter, time, or place
(3) Understanding, or the construction of ideas or concepts by a series of judgments

"Things" are outside of our mind. "Forms" (or perceptions of things) are brought into the mind through the senses. These forms are disconnected from matter, time, and space and can be manipulated abstractly to produce ideas or concepts. These ideas are then tested by a series of judgments which lead to a more secure understanding.

Will
(Choice)

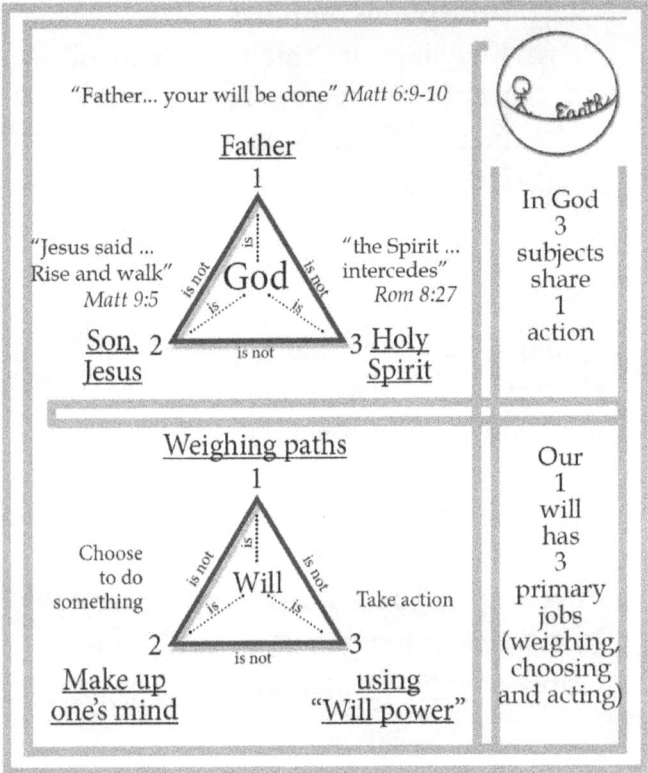

"Father... your will be done" *Matt 6:9-10*

Father
1

"Jesus said ... Rise and walk" *Matt 9:5*

is not · is · is not

God

is · is

is not

Son, 2
Jesus

3 Holy
Spirit

"the Spirit ... intercedes" *Rom 8:27*

In God
3
subjects
share
1
action

Weighing paths
1

Choose
to do
something

is not · is · is not

Will

is · is

is not

2

Make up
one's mind

3

using
"Will power"

Take action

Our
1
will
has
3
primary
jobs
(weighing,
choosing
and acting)

The will seeks the good as presented to it by the intellect. The job of the will is to choose among perceived goods and act upon those choices.

The will chooses a good; and a moral virtue begins. The will chooses something evil; and a moral evil begins.

Moral virtues and moral evils eventually become good habits or bad habits.

Knowing

"Father, the one seeing in secret ..."
Matt 6:4

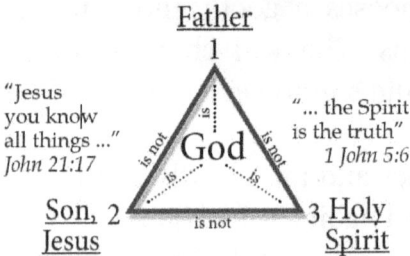

Father
1

"Jesus
you know
all things ..."
John 21:17

"... the Spirit
is the truth"
1 John 5:6

is

is not   is not

God

is   is

Son, 2 —————— 3 Holy
Jesus   is not   Spirit

In God
3
subjects
share
1
knowledge

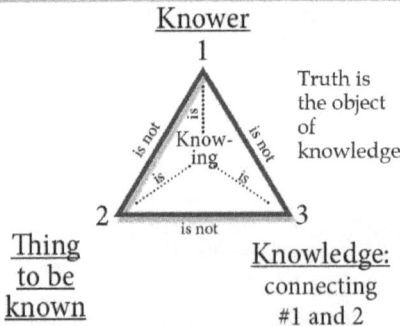

Knower
1

Truth is
the object
of
knowledge

is

is not   is not

Know-
ing

is   is

2   3
is not

Thing
to be
known

Knowledge:
connecting
#1 and 2

In us
1
knowing
experience
involves
3
parts
(knower,
object and
knowledge)

48

When we understand something well, or learn something perfectly, we and it become one. This situation mirrors the relationship between God the Father and His Word, God the Son (Jesus).

I (Jesus) and the Father are one.

John 10:30

Speech

"In the beginning was the Word,
and the Word was with God (the Father)"
John 1:1; 14:26

"... the Word
became flesh
(Jesus) and we
saw his glory"
"I (Jesus)
came forth
out of the
Father"
*John 1:14;
16:28*

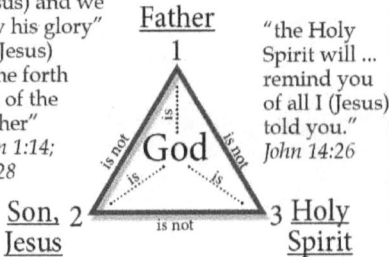

"the Holy
Spirit will ...
remind you
of all I (Jesus)
told you."
John 14:26

Father
1

God

is

is not   *is not*

is   *is*

Son,
Jesus
2

is not

3 ### Holy
Spirit

In God
3
subjects
share
1
word

Who I am & what I know of my
world, is defined by word.

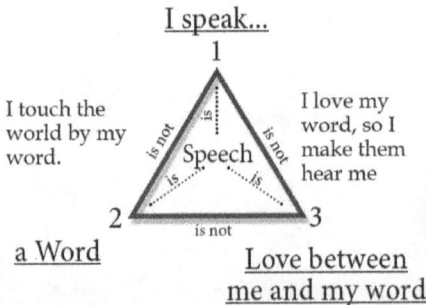

I speak...
1

I touch the
world by my
word.

I love my
word, so I
make them
hear me

Speech

is

is not   *is not*

is   *is*

2
a Word

is not

3
Love between
me and my word

In me
3
elements
(speaker,
word and
love)
make up
1
speech
event

Roger Skrenes

In my speech are three key elements:

(1) me, the speaker
(2) my word, which defines me, and
(3) my love for my word

This third element, love for my word, is sometimes demonstrated when I "cut another person off," while they are speaking — to make sure that my word gets out and that I am decisively heard.

Inner Conversation

"I (Jesus) did not speak of myself but the Father having sent me has given me...what to say." *John 12:49*

Father
1

"... my teaching is not mine, but the (Father's) who sent me" *John 7:16*

"... the things of God no one has known, except the Spirit of God" *1 Cor 2:11*

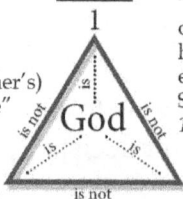

is not   is   is not

God

is   is

Son, 2 Jesus   is not   3 ### Holy Spirit

In God 3 subjects share 1 conversation

In my mind I express myself in words

Speaker
1

I listen to myself and evaluate my thoughts

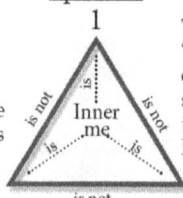

There is the 'spirit'-ed love connecting my speaker-self to my listener-self

is not   is   is not

Inner me

is   is

Listener   2   is not   3 ### Connecting Love

In us 3 subjects (speaker, listener and love) share 1 conversation

At night my "speaker" self sometimes talks without my knowing it. Someone tells me what I said when my "listener" self was asleep

The Trinity is present in the words of
Isaiah 61:1

The (1) Spirit of the (2) Lord Yahweh
(God the Father) is on (3) Me (God the
Son), to preach good news to the poor.
He has sent me ... to
proclaim liberty to captives ...
Isaiah 61:1

In the NT, Jesus read these words from
Isaiah 61:1 while in the synagogue at
Nazareth to begin his public ministry.

The (1) Spirit of the (2) Lord (God
the Father), is upon Me (God the Son),
whereupon He anointed Me to
evangelize the poor. He has sent Me to
proclaim release of captives ...
Luke 4:18

Earlier, at the Jordan River, God the
Father had "anointed" Jesus with the
Spirit — confirming his triune identity.
Luke 3:21-22

Self-Image

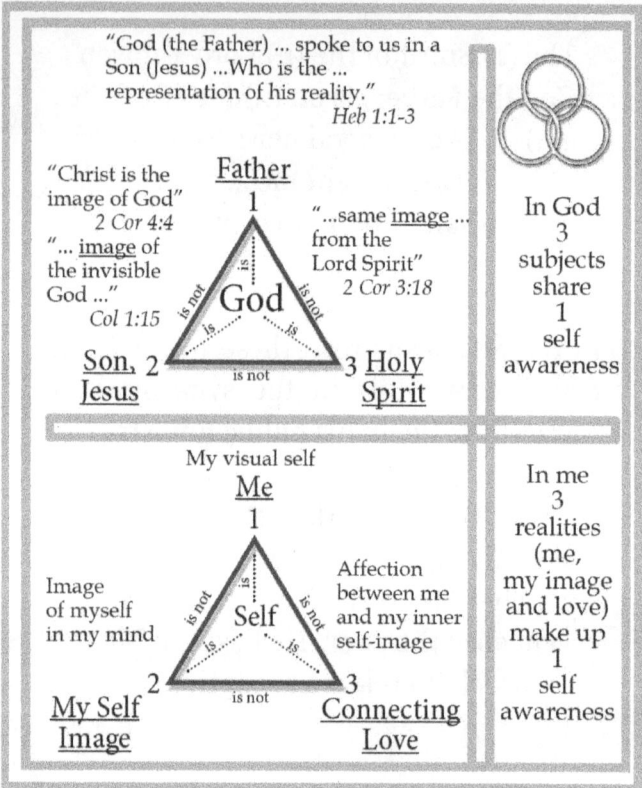

"God (the Father) ... spoke to us in a Son (Jesus) ...Who is the ... representation of his reality."
Heb 1:1-3

"Christ is the image of God"
2 Cor 4:4
"... image of the invisible God ..."
Col 1:15

Father
1

"...same image ... from the Lord Spirit"
2 Cor 3:18

is
is not
God
is not
is
is

Son, 2
Jesus

is not

3 Holy
Spirit

In God
3
subjects
share
1
self
awareness

My visual self
Me
1

Image of myself in my mind

is
is not
Self
is not
is

Affection between me and my inner self-image

2
My Self
Image

is not

3
Connecting
Love

In me
3
realities
(me,
my image
and love)
make up
1
self
awareness

"Me," as others see me, and the mental image I have of myself are separate realities:

Me (1) is a material, visual reality. My self-image (2) exists only in my mind.

Furthermore, there is a love (3) between

the material image I see when I look in the mirror, and my inner self-image or idea I have of myself.

IV. Friendship

Conversation

Friendly
conversation joins
people together.

"There came (the Father's) voice... 'This is My Son...'"
Mark 9:7

In God 3 subjects share 1 conversation

Father
1

"... you (Father) hear me always ..."
John 11:42

"Spirit appeals..."
Rom 8:26

is not
is
God
is not
is
is not

Son, 2
Jesus

3 Holy
Spirit

Talker #1
1

Conversation topics:
a book,
a movie,
a ballgame,
etc.

In conversation 3 elements become as 1

is not
is
Conversa-
tion
is not
is
is not

Talker #2
2

3
Topic:
that unites #1 and 2

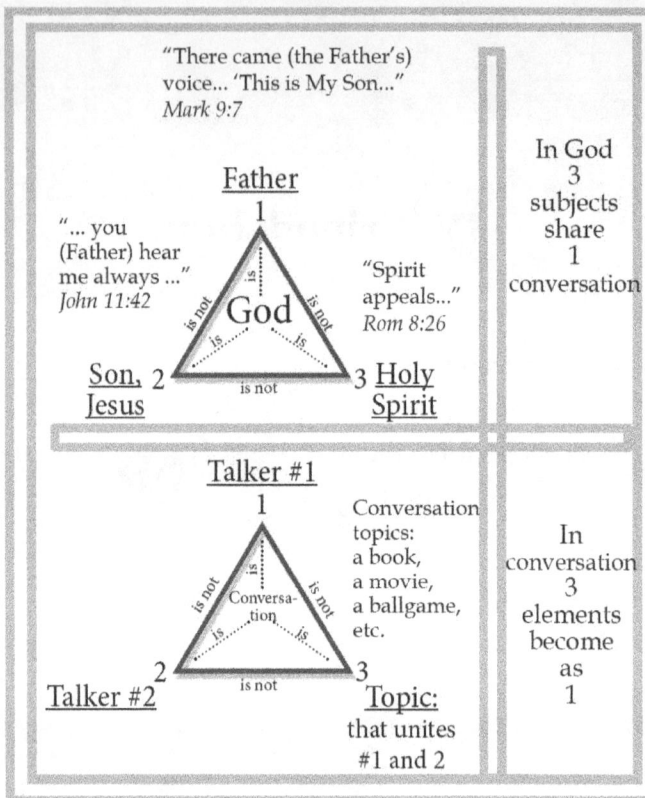

In conversation people talk. When they talk, they must talk about something. They may discuss many things in a long conversation, but usually only one at a time. This being so, a conversation is a three-some action: Two speakers + one topic (3-in-1); and is an image of the triune God.

Friendship

We cannot remain in relation to another person unless there is something else — a third element. This bonding "glue" could be the same career; parenting or church; sports (tennis, golf, etc.); or anything that — "we have in common."

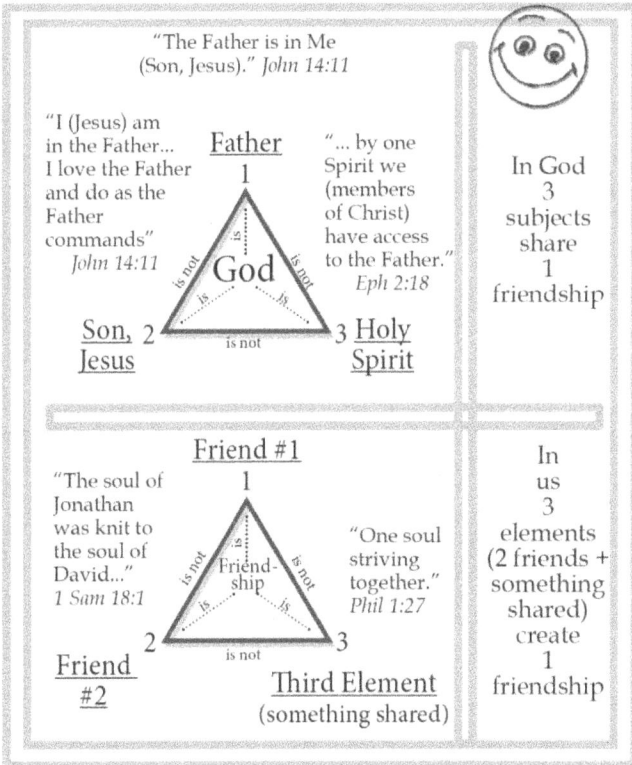

"The Father is in Me (Son, Jesus)." *John 14:11*

"I (Jesus) am in the Father... I love the Father and do as the Father commands" *John 14:11*

Father
1

"... by one Spirit we (members of Christ) have access to the Father." *Eph 2:18*

God
is not / *is* / *is not*
is

Son, Jesus 2 — *is not* — 3 **Holy Spirit**

In God
3
subjects
share
1
friendship

"The soul of Jonathan was knit to the soul of David..." *1 Sam 18:1*

Friend #1
1

Friend-ship
is not / *is* / *is not*
is

"One soul striving together." *Phil 1:27*

Friend #2 2 — *is not* — 3 **Third Element**
(something shared)

In us
3
elements
(2 friends + something shared)
create
1
friendship

59

God was not alone before He created the world. He was not a "loner."

Yahweh (the Father) possessed
Me (the Word) in the beginning
of His ways, before His works ...
I was there from the beginning
... In His preparing the heavens I was there
... in His setting limits for the sea ...
I was at His side a workman ...
I was His delight day by day ...

Proverbs 8:22-31

The love between God as Father and
His Word, God the Son, shows forth.
The Holy Spirit is
the bond of that love.
The NT says that "God is love.

1 John 4:8

Friends

"... let us love one another because love is of God ..." *1 John 4:7*

Father
1

"I (Jesus) love the Father ..." *John 14:31*

God

is · is · is not · is not · is not

Son, 2 — is not — 3 Holy
Jesus · · · · · · · · Spirit

"the fruit of the Spirit is love ..." *Gal 5:22*

In God
3
subjects
share
1
Love

Friend
1

"Your friend is as your own soul." *Deut 13:6*

One Soul

is · is · is not · is not · is

2 — is not — 3
Friend · · · · · · · Friend

"Jonathan loved David as his own soul." *1 Sam 18:1*

3
friends
are as
1
soul

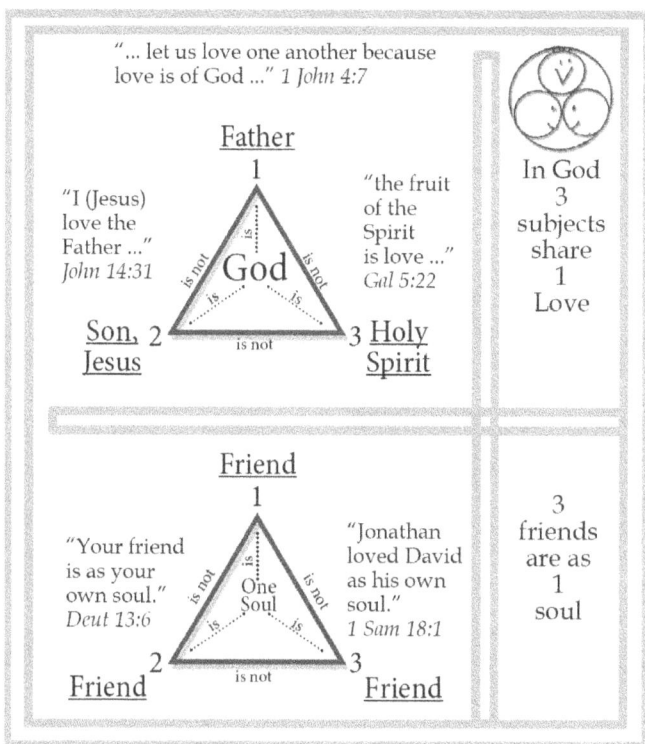

In God three subjects share one consciousness. By contrast, good friends have separate consciousnesses which in content approach one another. In other words, they share similar interests (a function of the intellect) and similar loves (a function of the will). They share, as if they were one soul, though they are separate persons.

V. Love

Being "in love"

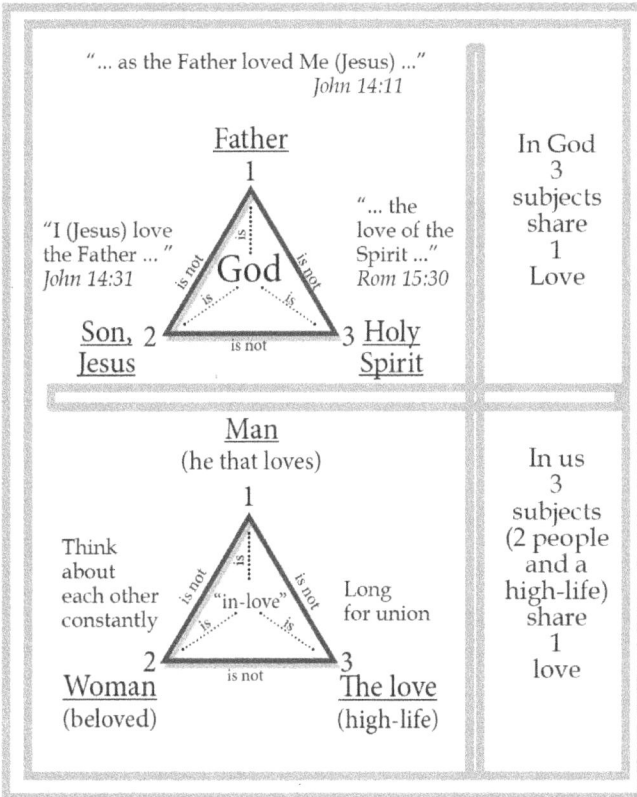

"... as the Father loved Me (Jesus) ..."
John 14:11

Father
1

"I (Jesus) love
the Father ... "
John 14:31

"... the
love of the
Spirit ..."
Rom 15:30

God

is

is not

is not

is

is

is not

Son, 2
Jesus

3 Holy
Spirit

In God
3
subjects
share
1
Love

Man
(he that loves)
1

Think
about
each other
constantly

"in-love"

Long
for union

is

is not

is not

is

is

is not

2
Woman
(beloved)

3
The love
(high-life)

In us
3
subjects
(2 people
and a
high-life)
share
1
love

Being in love is a peak-experience, and heaven-like.

Time stops. Space between lovers diminishes. Energy is doubled. The older person feels younger and the younger person feels wise.

When speaking with others, the lovers appear to be only half there. Their soul is with the other person, and they long for union with them.

The Greeks expressed this phenomenon by speaking of one's "better half."

Roger Skrenes

Marriage

"I (Jesus) am not alone, because the Father is with me." *John 16:32*

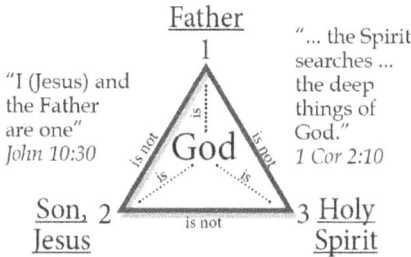

Father
1

"... the Spirit searches ... the deep things of God."
1 Cor 2:10

"I (Jesus) and the Father are one"
John 10:30

is not / is
God
is not

Son, 2
Jesus

is not

3 Holy
Spirit

In God
3
subjects
share
1
Bond

Physical
attraction
(passion)

Sensing

1
Romance ↓
Marriage
Sex

2 ↗ ↖ 3

Companions

In
marriage
3
facets
lead to
1
bond

Friendship
(intimacy)

Commitment
(loyalty)

Understanding

Judgement

65

The Bible says, "God is love."

1 John 4:16

It also says that each person is created in God's image.

Gen 1:26

Love is patient, love is kind, love is
not jealous or boastful or arrogant.
Love does not insist on its own way;
it is not irritable or resentful.

1 Cor 13:4-5

Sacred Marriage

In marriage there is the husband, wife, and God who joins them together.

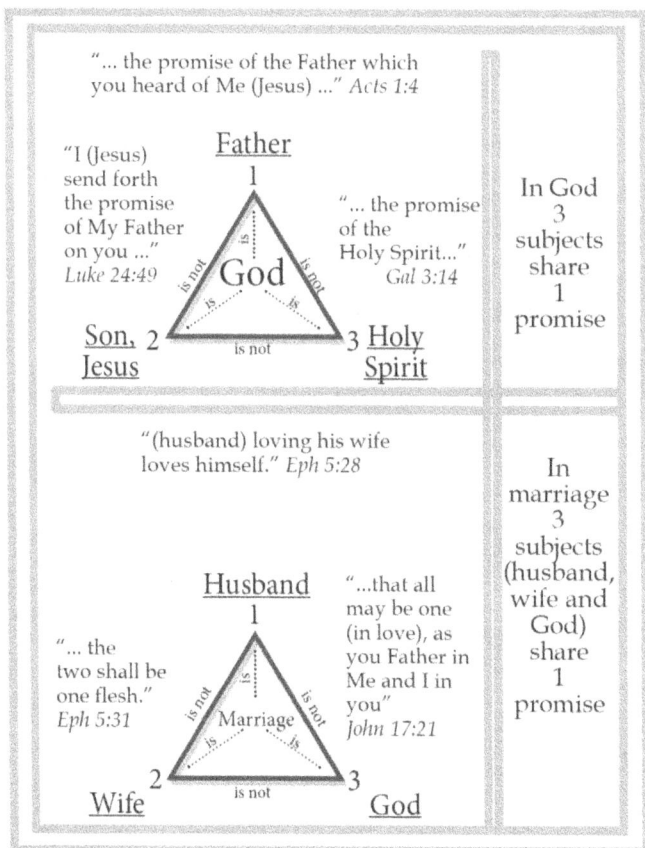

"... the promise of the Father which you heard of Me (Jesus) ..." *Acts 1:4*

"I (Jesus) send forth the promise of My Father on you ..." *Luke 24:49*

"... the promise of the Holy Spirit..." *Gal 3:14*

Father
1

is not · is not

God

is not

Son, 2
Jesus

is not

3 ### Holy
Spirit

In God
3
subjects
share
1
promise

"(husband) loving his wife loves himself." *Eph 5:28*

"... the two shall be one flesh." *Eph 5:31*

"...that all may be one (in love), as you Father in Me and I in you" *John 17:21*

Husband
1

is not · is not

Marriage

is not

2
Wife

is not

3
God

In
marriage
3
subjects
(husband,
wife and
God)
share
1
promise

Marriage is like the relationship between Christ and His Church. The husband is like Christ; the wife is like the Church. (*Eph 5:23-24*) The husband loves his wife as Christ loved the Church and gave Himself up on behalf of it.

Eph 5:25

The wife defers to her husband as the church submits to Christ.

Eph 5:22

Christ and the church are in reality one, as the Mystical Body.

Ephesians 1:23; 1 Cor 12:27; Acts 9:4-5

Family

"God is love." *1 John 4:8*
"The Father loved the Son ...
before the foundation of the world.."
John 17:24

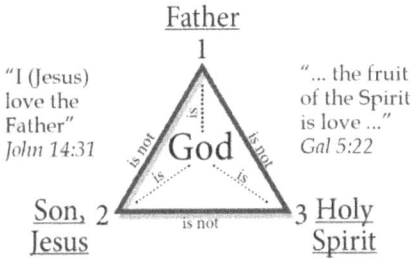

In God
3
subjects
share
1
Love

Father
1

"I (Jesus)
love the
Father"
John 14:31

God

"... the fruit
of the Spirit
is love ..."
Gal 5:22

is not   is not

is   is

is not

Son, 2   3 Holy
Jesus   Spirit

The husband earns money
to support the family

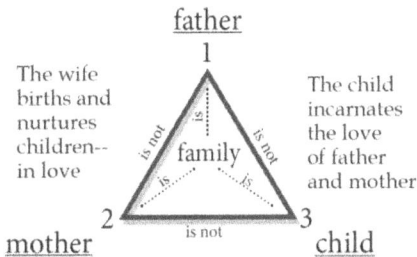

In the
family
3
subjects
share
1
Love

father
1

The wife
births and
nurtures
children--
in love

family

The child
incarnates
the love
of father
and mother

is not   is not

is   is

is not

2   3
mother   child

St. Joseph was not at the foot of the cross. Mary was probably a widow and certainly without other children. To ensure that Mary would have a family when He was gone, Jesus named the Apostle John for this loving work.

Then He said to the disciple (John):

"Behold, your (new) mother!";
and from that hour the disciple
took her to his own (home)."
John 19:27

Thus, Jesus taught us that everyone should be anchored within the family where there is love.

VI. Family Dynamics

Family

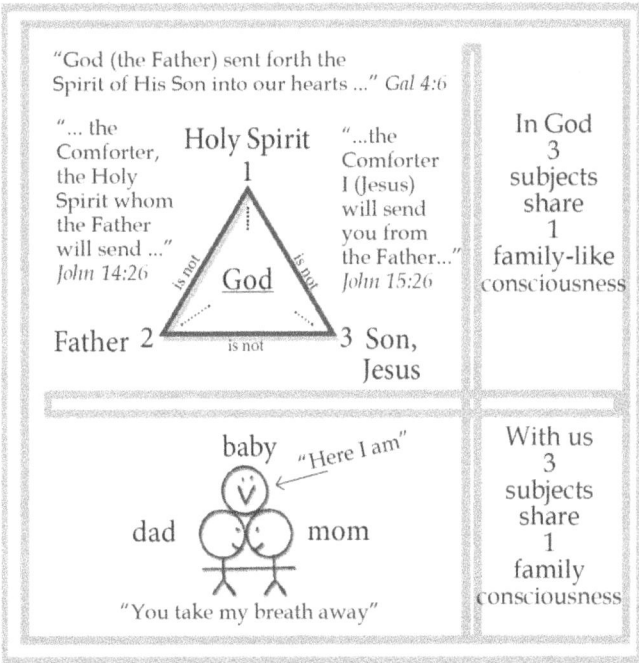

"God (the Father) sent forth the Spirit of His Son into our hearts ..." *Gal 4:6*

"... the Comforter, the Holy Spirit whom the Father will send ..." *John 14:26*

Holy Spirit 1

"...the Comforter I (Jesus) will send you from the Father..." *John 15:26*

is not   God   is not

Father 2   is not   3 Son, Jesus

In God 3 subjects share 1 family-like consciousness

baby   "Here I am"

dad   mom

"You take my breath away"

With us 3 subjects share 1 family consciousness

In God, three subjects share one divine nature. The Holy Spirit proceeds *eternally* from the indwelling love of the Father and Son. By analogy, each

71

human child proceeds *in time* from the indwelling love of the husband and wife.

Father and Son

"All things were delivered to me (Jesus) by my Father ..." *Luke 10:22*

Father
1

Divine
Nature

is

is not   is not

is

is not

Son, 2   3 Holy
Jesus   Spirit

"I know
Him (the Father)
because I am
from Him ..."
John 7:29

"God
(the Father)
sent forth
the Spirit of
His Son ..."
Gal 4:6

In God
3
relations
share
1
divine
nature

father
1

human
nature

is

is not   is not

is

is not

son   love

love

a 'likeness'
of nature
with my
father

The bond,
or "holy
spirit"
between
father
and son

2
related
persons
share
1
human
nature

In God there is one *divine nature* shared by Father and Son.

In the human father and son there is one *human nature* shared.

The Son was eternally begotten, but not made (that is, not created).

However, a human son is made or created in time.

Life Roles

"I (the Word, or Son) came forth out of the Father." *John 16:28*

Father
1

"I (Jesus) live through the Father." *John 6:57*

"God sent forth the Spirit of his Son ... crying 'abba Father'." *Gal 4:6*

is
is not
is not
God
is
is
is not

Son, 2 Jesus

3 Holy Spirit

In God
3 subjects share 1 consciousness

My children think of me as their dad (not as a teacher)

husband
dad teacher

father role
1

My wife thinks of me as her husband (not as her father or teacher)

My students think of me as their teacher (not as their father)

is not
is
Me
is
is not
is
is not

2
husband role

3
job role

is not

In us
3 roles share 1 consciousness

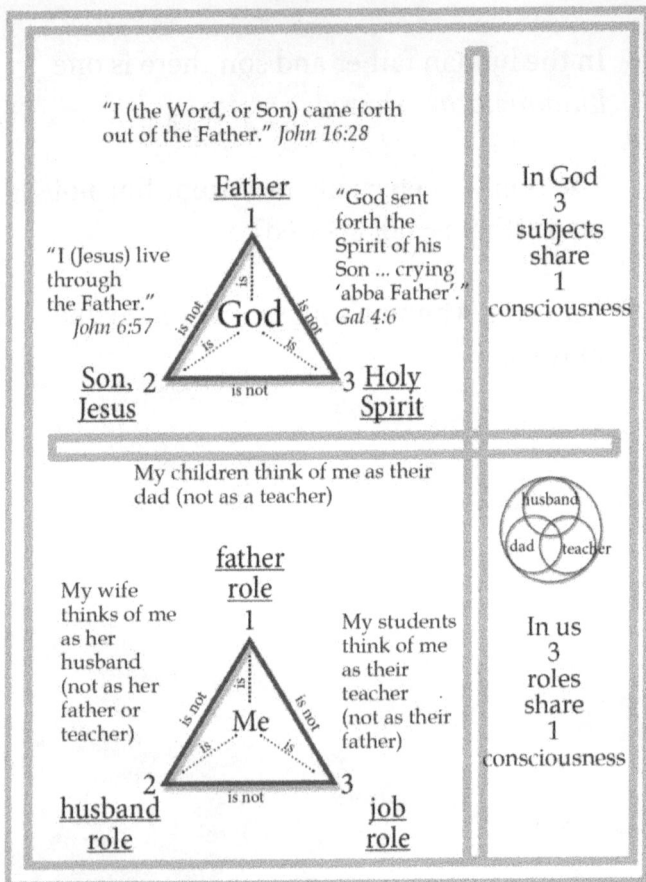

In our adult life there are three key roles. For a male, these roles are often as husband, father, and worker. In these roles we live as one person. These roles are not confused within us. We can be talking with our spouse and our child simultaneously. We can be at work showing a son how our job is done. We remain as one. A healthy life is perceived as a whole rather than in its several parts. This is an image of the Triune God.

See *Genesis 1:27*

Empty Nest

Children grow up and leave home. When this occurs, parents usually fill the gap with "something else." They "take up" a new activity that binds them together.

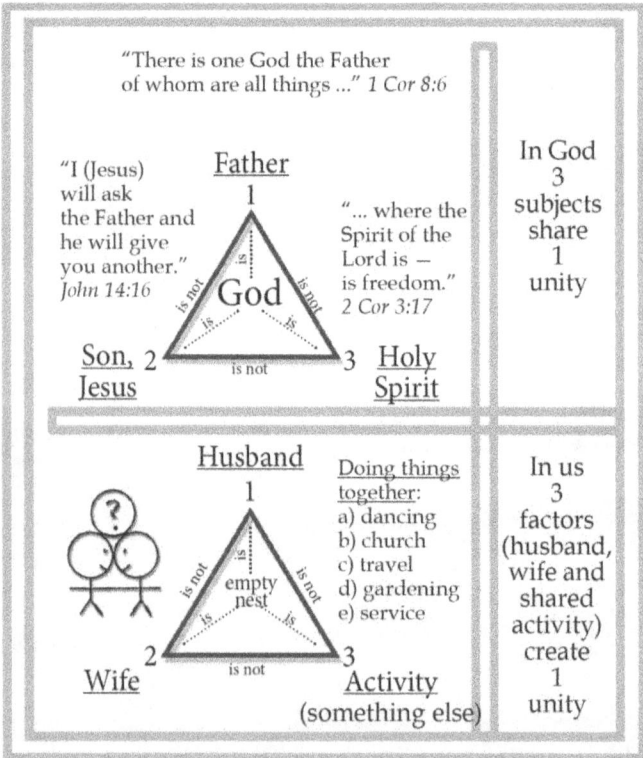

"There is one God the Father of whom are all things ..." *1 Cor 8:6*

"I (Jesus) will ask the Father and he will give you another." *John 14:16*

Father
1
God
is not
is not
is not
is not

"... where the Spirit of the Lord is — is freedom." *2 Cor 3:17*

Son, 2
Jesus

3 Holy
Spirit

In God
3
subjects
share
1
unity

Husband
1
empty nest
is not
is not
is not
is not

Doing things together:
a) dancing
b) church
c) travel
d) gardening
e) service

Wife
2

3
Activity
(something else)

In us
3
factors
(husband, wife and shared activity)
create
1
unity

Relationships are made possible by a "third factor." This could be children, home-making, sports, movies, dancing, a travel destination, college program, church service, or any other activity when shared.

Two people alone are separated. To be related they must become "triune."

They need a common "spirit" or shared experience to tie them together. To remain in relation to each other, they must refer to "something else."

Pets

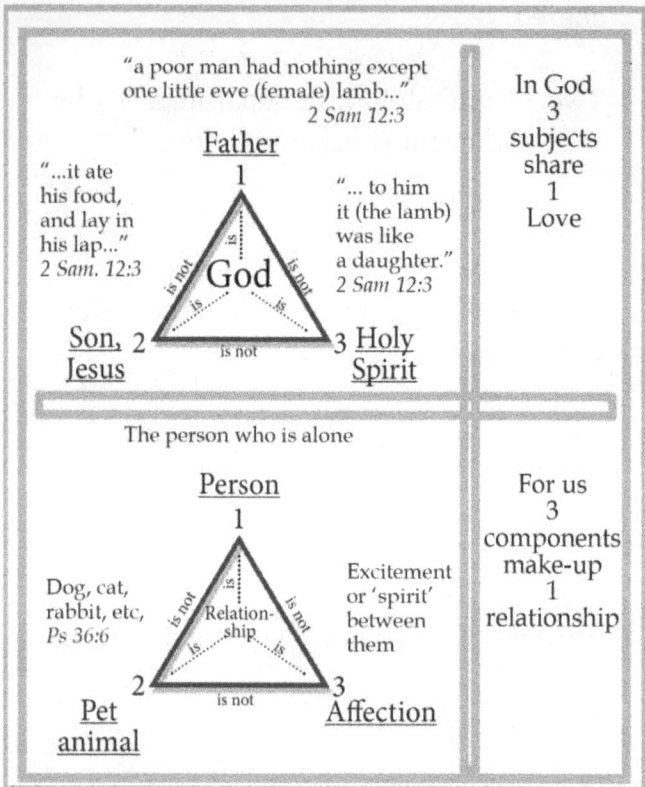

"a poor man had nothing except one little ewe (female) lamb..."
2 Sam 12:3

In God
3
subjects
share
1
Love

"...it ate his food, and lay in his lap..."
2 Sam. 12:3

"... to him it (the lamb) was like a daughter."
2 Sam 12:3

Father
1
God
is
is not
is not
is
is not

Son, 2
Jesus

3 Holy
Spirit

The person who is alone

For us
3
components
make-up
1
relationship

Dog, cat, rabbit, etc,
Ps 36:6

Excitement or 'spirit' between them

Person
1
Relation-ship
is
is not
is not
is
is not

Pet
animal 2

3
Affection

Roger Skrenes

"God is love"

1 John 4:8

We are created in God's image.

Gen 1:26

We need someone or something to love. For some this may involve a pet animal. Will some animals be in Heaven with their owners? Notice the following verse from the Bible:

O God, you deliver man and animal.

Psalm 36:6

VII. Human Work

Work

The boss and the employee speak of a third thing — the job. The job binds them together "at work."

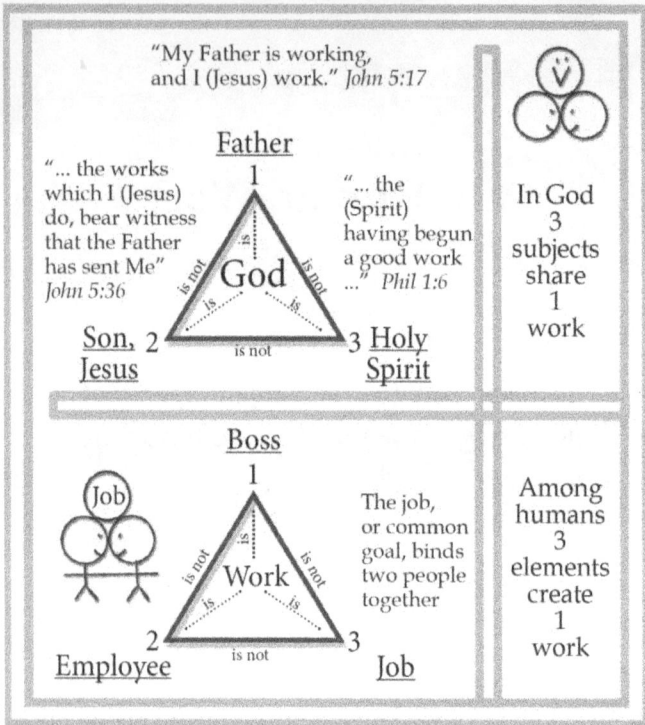

"My Father is working, and I (Jesus) work." *John 5:17*

Father
1

"... the works which I (Jesus) do, bear witness that the Father has sent Me" *John 5:36*

God

"... the (Spirit) having begun a good work ..." *Phil 1:6*

is not / is / is not

is / is not / is

Son, Jesus
2

is not

3 Holy Spirit

In God
3 subjects share
1 work

Boss
1

Work

The job, or common goal, binds two people together

Among humans
3 elements create
1 work

Job

is not / is / is not

is / is not / is

Employee
2

is not

3 Job

Work takes its meaning from God.
The heavens declare His glory
and were made by His fingers.
Psalms 8:3; 19:1

As a worker God, is "not faint
nor does he grow weary; there is
no searching to His understanding."
Isaiah 40:28

82

Research

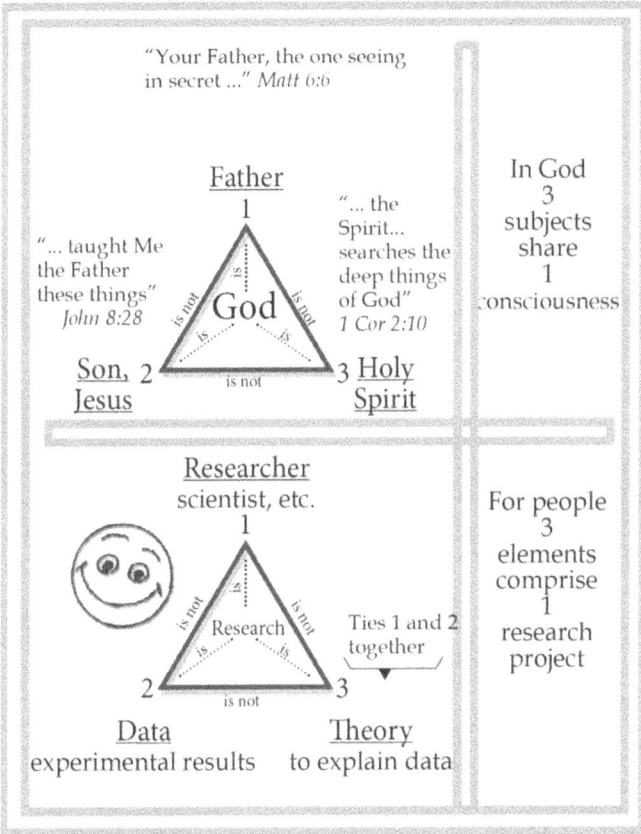

"Your Father, the one seeing in secret ..." *Matt 6:6*

Father
1

"... the Spirit... searches the deep things of God" *1 Cor 2:10*

"... taught Me the Father these things" *John 8:28*

God

is / is not / is not / is / is not

Son, 2
Jesus

3 Holy
Spirit

In God
3
subjects
share
1
consciousness

Researcher
scientist, etc.
1

is / is not / is not

Research

is / is not

2

3

Ties 1 and 2
together

Data
experimental results

Theory
to explain data

For people
3
elements
comprise
1
research
project

Research looks at God's creation and tries to understand its many parts. Its first task is to gather factual information called data. Then a theory is developed which provides some insight into this

83

data and indirectly into the mind of God. Such an effort honors the Creator.

Physical Science

In God: The Father, Son, and Holy Spirit are relationally one. In physical science: Chemistry, physics and math are also.

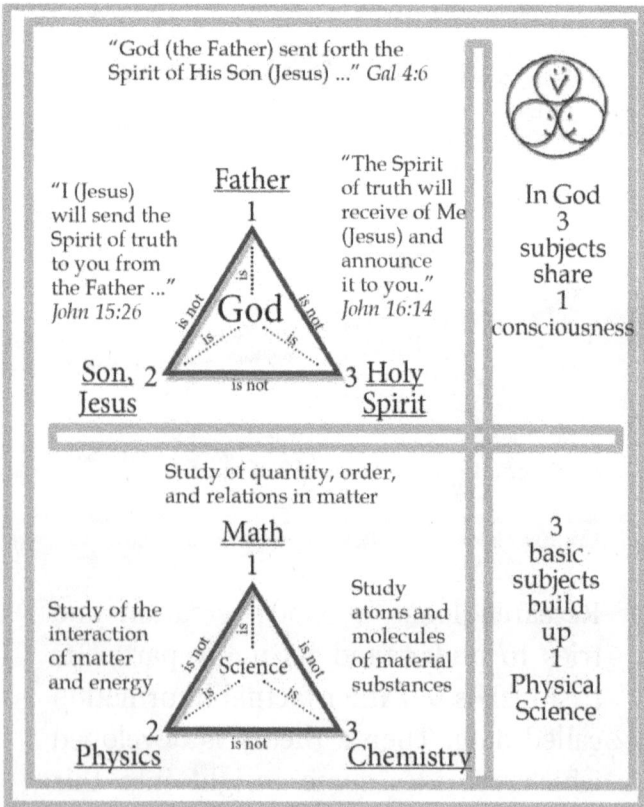

"God (the Father) sent forth the Spirit of His Son (Jesus) ..." *Gal 4:6*

"I (Jesus) will send the Spirit of truth to you from the Father ..." *John 15:26*

"The Spirit of truth will receive of Me (Jesus) and announce it to you." *John 16:14*

Father
1

God

is not   is   is   is not

is   is

Son, 2 —— is not —— 3 Holy
Jesus   Spirit

In God
3
subjects
share
1
consciousness

Study of quantity, order, and relations in matter

Math
1

Science

is not   is   is   is not

is   is

Physics 2 —— is not —— 3 Chemistry

Study of the interaction of matter and energy

Study atoms and molecules of material substances

3
basic
subjects
build
up
1
Physical
Science

Triune God

The three subjects in God share one divine nature. Therefore, God is one.

Deuteronomy 6:4

Jesus is the "image" of the Father, but not the Father.

Colossians 1:15

Jesus speaks only the Father's word.

John 14:24

The Father sends the Spirit from Jesus.

Galatians 4:6

Jesus sends the "Spirit of truth" from the Father.

John 15:26

The Spirit speaks only the Word(s) of Jesus.

John 16:13

The Spirit is a living subject. For example, he can be sinned against.

Matt 12:34; Luke 12:10; Acts 5:3

Democratic Government

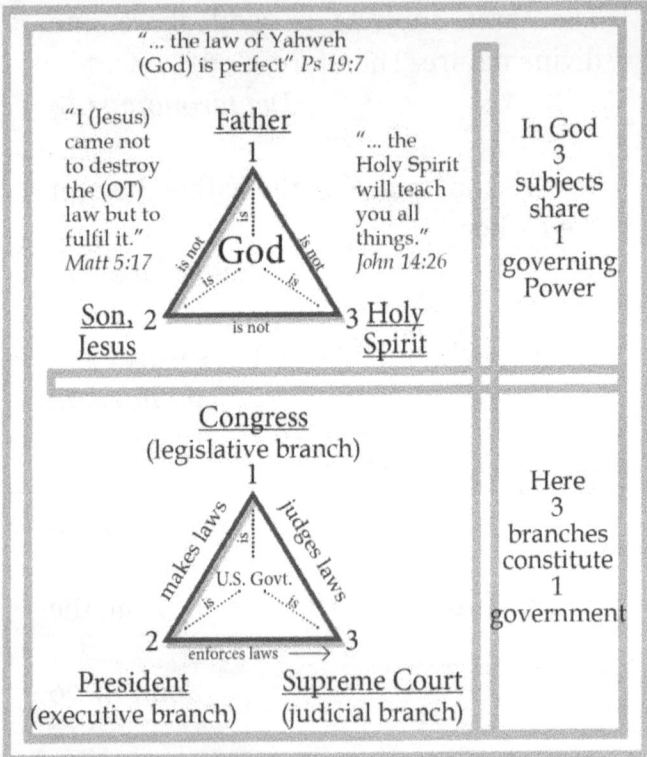

"... the law of Yahweh (God) is perfect" *Ps 19:7*

"I (Jesus) came not to destroy the (OT) law but to fulfil it." *Matt 5:17*

Father
1

is
is not   is not
God
is   is
is not

Son, 2   3 Holy
Jesus   Spirit

"... the Holy Spirit will teach you all things." *John 14:26*

In God
3
subjects
share
1
governing
Power

Congress
(legislative branch)
1

makes laws   judges laws
is
U.S. Govt.
is   is

2   3
enforces laws →

President
(executive branch)

Supreme Court
(judicial branch)

Here
3
branches
constitute
1
government

In the OT, God gave us law on Mt. Sinai: the Ten Commandments — a legislative function.

Exodus 20:1-17

In the NT, Jesus said he came to "fulfil" the OT law — an executive function.

Matthew 5:17

When departing, Jesus sent us the Holy Spirit to help us arrive at the truth – a judicial function.

John 16:13

Note: All governments have three basic powers: law making, executive and judicial functions. However, not all governments are democracies. In some governments, the three branches are not elected freely by the people.

VIII. Salvation

Incarnation

In the beginning was the Word, and the Word was with God (the Father), and the Word was God (the Son, Jesus) ... All things were made through him ... And the Word became flesh and dwelt among us, and we beheld his glory ...

John 1:1-3 &14

"The Angel said to Mary: 'The Holy Spirit will come unto you and the power of the Most High (Father) will overshadow you' Wherefore the holy thing (Jesus) being born, will be called Son of God." *Luke 1:35*

"... before they (Mary and Joseph) came together, she was found having a child in the womb by the Holy Spirit." *Matt 1:18*

In God 3 subjects share 1 Divine Being

"I (Jesus) came forth out of the Father, and have come into the world ..." *John 16:28*

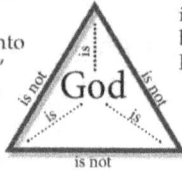

Old Testament

I [Christ] have not spoken in secret from the beginning. From the time of its being [the universe], I was there; and now the Lord Yahweh (the Father) has sent Me and His Spirit.

Isaiah 48:16

Roger Skrenes

New Testament

God (the Father) sent his only
begotten Son into the world in order
that we might live through him.

1 John 4:9

Faith

"...the Word which you hear is ... the Father's who sent me (Jesus)." *John 14:24*

"... the words which I (Jesus) say to you, I speak not from myself, but the Father remaining in Me ..." *John 14:10*

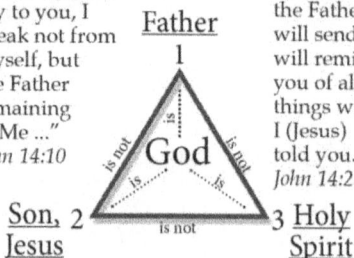

"... the Holy Spirit which the Father will send ... will remind you of all things which I (Jesus) told you." *John 14:26*

Father
1

is
is not   God   is not
is   is
is not

Son, 2   3 Holy
Jesus   Spirit

In God
3
subjects
share
1
message

"... beginning from Moses and all the prophets he (Jesus) explained to them the things concerning himself in all the (OT) scriptures." *Luke 24:27*

Remembering
God
1

"... growing in the ... knowledge of our Lord and savior Jesus Christ." *2 Pet 3:18*

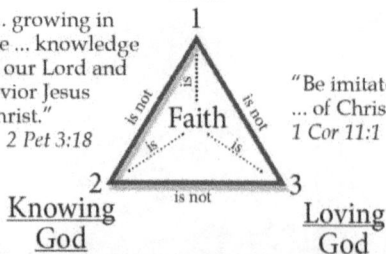

is
is not   Faith   is not
is   is

"Be imitators ... of Christ." *1 Cor 11:1*

is not

2   3
Knowing   Loving
God   God

In us
3
actions
lead
to
the
1
faith

92

Roger Skrenes

"Toward Him (Jesus), we had been running, or from him we had been running away; but all the while he was in the center of things."

Pillar of Fire
by Karl Stern, M.D.

Baptism

He that believes and is
baptized shall be saved.

Mark 16:16

Jesus himself baptized not,
but his disciples [did baptize].

John 4:2

"... he (John the Baptist) saw the Spirit of God coming down as a dove upon Him (Jesus), and behold the voice (of the Father) out of the heavens, said:
'This is My Son (Jesus)' " *Matt 3:16-17*

"... you ... baptize them in the name of the Father and of the Son and of the ... Holy spirit" *Matt 28:19*

Father
1

"(Jesus) is the one baptizing in Holy Spirit ..." *John 1:33*

God

is not   is not   is   is   is not

Son, 2 <u>Jesus</u>   3 <u>Holy Spirit</u>

In God
3
subjects
share
1
divine
action

"... one is born of water and the Spirit ... " *John 3:5*

He saved us, by the washing
of regeneration, and a
renewing of the Holy Spirit."

Titus 3:5

Your body is the temple

of the Holy Spirit... You are
washed (baptized) ... Your bodies
are members of Christ ...
1 Cor 6:11; 15:19

You were baptized into Christ.
Gal 3:27; Rom 6:3

[B]aptism now saves us ...
1 Peter 3:21

Eucharist

The Eucharized Bread is the certain Presence of Jesus in the Christian community.

"A little while and you will see me no more."
John 6:44

"As the living Father sent me (Jesus), and I live through the father... so he who eats me (the Eucharized Bread) will live through me." *John 6:57*

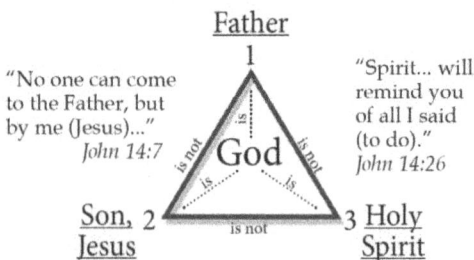

Father
1

"No one can come to the Father, but by me (Jesus)..."
John 14:7

is not is not

is is

God

"Spirit... will remind you of all I said (to do)."
John 14:26

Son, 2
Jesus

is not

3 Holy
Spirit

"I am the Bread of (eternal) life." *John 6:48*

"Take, eat: this Bread is my Body... which is given for you (hereafter)."
Mt 26:26; Luke 22:19

During his public life, Jesus promised
the following:

> Where two or three are gathered
> together in my name, there
> I Am in the middle of them.
> [literal English from the Greek]
> *Matthew 18:20*

This Presence is an external presence.
Jesus wanted to do even more! He
wanted to be internally Present in each
Christian. That is why, at the Last
Supper he gave himself in the Eucharist.

Church

"My Father will love him... We will come, and make our abode with him." *John 14:23*

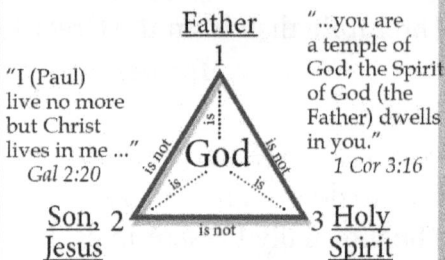

Father
1

"...you are a temple of God; the Spirit of God (the Father) dwells in you."
1 Cor 3:16

"I (Paul) live no more but Christ lives in me ..." *Gal 2:20*

God

is not

is

is not

is

is not

Son, Jesus
2

Holy Spirit
3

In God
3
subjects
share
1
Mission

"... your faith has saved you." *Luke 7:50*

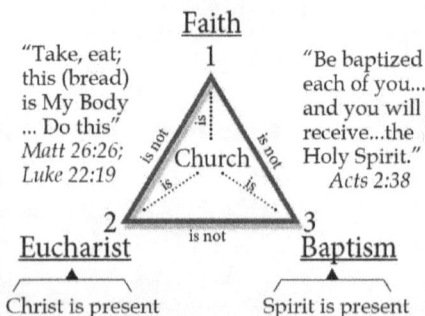

Faith
1

"Take, eat; this (bread) is My Body ... Do this" *Matt 26:26; Luke 22:19*

"Be baptized each of you... and you will receive...the Holy Spirit." *Acts 2:38*

Church

is not

is

is not

is

is not

Eucharist
2

Baptism
3

Christ is present

Spirit is present

3 actions
build
up
the
1
Church

In God three subjects possess one divine nature. They differ only by relations. For example, in *John 10:30* Jesus did not say: "I am the Father." Rather he said: "I and the Father are one."

The Holy Spirit is also a separate subject.

In *John 14:16*, Jesus says:

The Father will give you another Comforter ...

This comforting Spirit directs people *(Acts 15:28)* and can be sinned against. *(Matt 12:31; Luke 12:10; Acts 5:3)*.

Spiritual Gifts

The fruit of the Spirit is love, joy, peace,
long-suffering, kindness, goodness,
faithfulness ...

Gal 5:2

"(there is) one God the Father
of whom are all things..."   *1 Cor 8:6*

Father
1

"(there is) one
Lord Jesus
through whom
are all things..."
1 Cor 8:6

"there are
differences of
gifts but the
same (Holy)
Spirit... "
1 Cor 12:4

is
is not   God   is not
is   is
is not

Son, 2
Jesus

3 Holy
Spirit

In God
3
subjects
share
1
divine
work

Paul addressed these statements to new Christians at Corinth in Greece. Paul founded the church at Corinth in 51 AD, and worked there eighteen months. At the end of this period he was taken by his Jewish accusers before Lucius J. Gallio, governor of Achaia — a province of the Roman Empire. Gallio was the brother of the Roman philosopher Seneca (4 BC- 65 AD), an adviser to Emperor Nero. Gallio refused to proceed to trial against Paul. (*Acts 18, 12-17*)

The seat where Gallio heard Paul's case has been found in Corinth. Also, an inscription found at Delphi mentions Gallio as pro-consul of Achaia in the years 51-52 AD. Paul wrote his first letter to the Corinthians in 53 AD.

Prayer

Prayer is lifting the heart and mind to God.

"... when you pray, say: Father ..." *Luke 11:2*
"God the Father knows what things
you need before you ask for them." *Matt 6:8*

"... pray
unceasingly...
this is the will of
God (the Father)
in Christ Jesus ...
Do not quench
the Spirit ..."
1 Thess 5:17-19

Father
1

God

is

is

is not

is not

is

is not

Son, 2
Jesus

3 Holy
Spirit

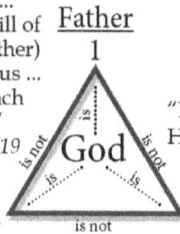

"Praying in the
Holy Spirit"
Jude 1:20

In God
3
subjects
share
1
voice

Each of the three subjects in God share one divine nature (or essence). That is why the Holy Spirit can be "Spirit of the Father" *(Matt 10:20)* and "Spirit of Jesus" *(Acts 16:7)*. The Holy Spirit is not a vital force of the Father and Son, but rather a real subject.

First, a vital force cannot be sinned against, as *Mark 3:29* shows: "Whoever blasphemes the Holy Spirit has no forgiveness."

Second, Jesus the "Son of man" is revealed alongside the Holy Spirit in *Matthew 12:32*.

Third, in *Acts 5:3-4*, Ananias lies to the Holy Spirit. Only a person (not a force) can be lied to.

Fourth, though "Spirit" (pneuma) is neuter in gender; "paraclete" (*Para kletos*), another name for the Holy Spirit, is masculine in gender. *John 14:16*

Resurrection

Each of the three subjects in God
was involved in the resurrection
of Jesus on Easter.

"... the Father of glory ... operated in Christ,
raising him from the dead." *Eph 1:17*
"Christ was raised from the dead
through the glory of the Father ..." *Rom 6:4*

"... in three days
I will raise it
(my body)."
John 2:19
"I have authority
to take it (up again)."
John 10:18

Father
1

"the Spirit
...raised
Jesus ..."
Rom 8:11

God

Son, 2
Jesus

is not

3 Holy
Spirit

In God
3
subjects
share
1
power

God creates by truth and love. That is
why our mind (intellect) is ordered to
truth, and our heart (will) is ordered to
love.

Roger Skrenes

Christian Resurrection

Each of the three subjects in God is involved in the resurrection of a person.

"As the Father raises the dead ... so also the Son (Jesus) ..." *John 5:21*

"I (Jesus) am the resurrection and the life; the one believing in me even if he should die will live." *John 11:25*

Father
1

God

Son, 2
Jesus

is not

3 **Holy**
Spirit

"... God will raise your mortal bodies through His Spirit indwelling in you." *Rom 8:11*

In God
3
subjects
share
1
power

Jesus took Peter, James and John ... and led them up a high mountain. And there he was transfigured [transformed] before them; his face shone like the sun, and his garments became white as light. And, there appeared to them Moses [1250 BC] and Elijah [850 BC] talking with Jesus.

Matt 17:1-3

105

Notice that Moses and Elijah came from heaven to speak with Jesus. These two heavenly men had walked upon the earth hundreds of years before this event took place. They are examples of two people alive beyond death, alive after their stay upon this planet.

IX. Powers of God

Omnipresent God

God is present in all places and in all things.

"God ... is lord of heaven and earth..." *Acts 17:24*
"... the one God and Father is over all ... and in all." *Eph 4:6*

"I (Jesus) am with you all days ..." *Matt 28:20; 18:20*

Father
1

"... where shall I go from your Spirit ..." *Ps 139:7*

is not

God

is

is not

Son, 2
Jesus

is not

3 Holy
Spirit

In God
3
subjects
share
1
Presence

"... his body ... fills all things ..." *Eph 1:23*
"Christ is ... in all (things)." *Col 3:11*

God is not bound in space or by time. God is not bound to one space. He is present in multiple locations simultaneously.

Time is also no problem for God because God has no time. God is everywhere at the same time.

Omnipotent God

God is almighty, or all-powerful. He rules all things outside Himself which He brought into existence and holds in existence.

"I am God the Almighty" *Gen 17:1*
"God (the Father) the one having made the world and all things in it ..." *Acts 17:24*

Father
1

"Christs is the power of God." *1 Cor 1:24*

"... by power of the Spirit ..." *Rom 15:13; 15:19*

God

is not   is   is not

Son, 2   is not   3 Holy
Jesus   Spirit

In God
3
subjects
share
1
power

"A Son (Jesus) ... through whom He (the Father) made the ages ... by the Word of His power." *Heb 1:2-3*

Jesus raised three people from the dead, walked on water, stilled a storm, fed 5000 people with five loaves of bread and two fish, and cured thousands of people who were seriously ill.

Power went forth from Him
and it cured all.

Luke 6:19

Omniscient God

Omniscience means that God is all-knowing. He knows everything that happened in the past, everything happening now throughout the universe, and everything that will happen in the future.

"The eyes of Yahweh are in every place, watching... *Prov 15:3*
"... there is no creature not manifest before him, but all things are naked and have been laid open to his eyes." *Heb 4:13*

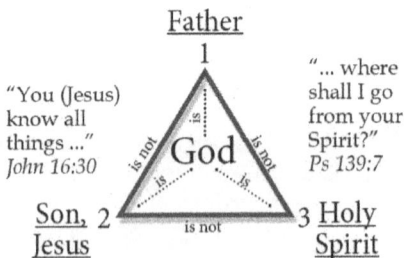

Father
1

"You (Jesus) know all things ..." *John 16:30*

is
is not
God
is not
is
is not

Son, 2
Jesus

is not

3 Holy Spirit

"... where shall I go from your Spirit?" *Ps 139:7*

"... neither does anyone fully know the Father, except the Son (Jesus) ..." *Matt 11:27*

"... the Spirit searches all things ..." *1 Cor 2:10*

In God
3
subjects
share
1
omniscience

Does God not see my ways
and count all my steps?

Job 31:4

Roger Skrenes

The 90-year-old Sarah laughed to
herself in her tent after God told her
she would give birth. God
nonetheless saw her laugh!
Gen 18:10-15

King David covered up his murder of
Uriah! However God sent Nathan
to say: "You are the man!"
2 Sam 11:1-12

Eternal God

God is beyond time. There never was a time when God did not exist. There never will be a time when God stops existing. In Jesus we see this timeless God.

"Yahweh reigns forever and ever."
Exod 15:18; Ps 102:27
"... the goings of eternity are to Him .."
Heb 3:6
"... eternal life was with the Father ..."
1 John 1:2

"Father ...
I had glory
with you
before the
world was."
John 17:5

Father
1

God

is not

is not

is not

is not

is

is

Son, 2
Jesus

3 Holy
Spirit

"... through
the eternal
Spirit ..."
Heb 9:14

In God
3
subjects
share
1
eternal
life

"... life eternal, was manifested
to us (in Jesus)" *1 John 1:2*

In Jesus we see the timeless God. Jesus was the God of Abraham even though Abraham lived on this planet 1600 years before Jesus. Yet, Jesus says,

"Before Abraham became, I Am."
John 8:58

Roger Skrenes

What was from the beginning we
have heard and have seen with our
eyes. We watched and our hands
touched the Word of life [Jesus].
For this life was manifested, and
we have seen it and bear witness...
eternal life that was with the Father,
and was manifested to us.

1 John 1:1-2

Immutable God

Immutability means not changing. Though God acts in time, His essence, attributes and promises never change.

"I Yahweh do not change ..." *Mal 3:6*
"... the Father ... with whom change or ... turning has no place." *James 1:17*

In God 3 subjects share 1 truth

Father 1

"Jesus Christ is the same yesterday and today and into the ages. *Heb 13:8*

is not · is · is not
is · God · is
is not

"...the Spirit of truth will guide you into all the truth ..." *John 16:13*

Son, 2   3 Holy
Jesus   Spirit

"Your Word is settled forever in Heaven." *Ps 119:89*

God has not evolved, grown, or improved. Jesus went through developmental changes in his human nature (humanness); but not in his divine nature (deity). Jesus Christ is the same yesterday, today, and forever.

James 1:17

One God

God has one divine nature. Because of this the Father is present in the Son and in the Holy Spirit.

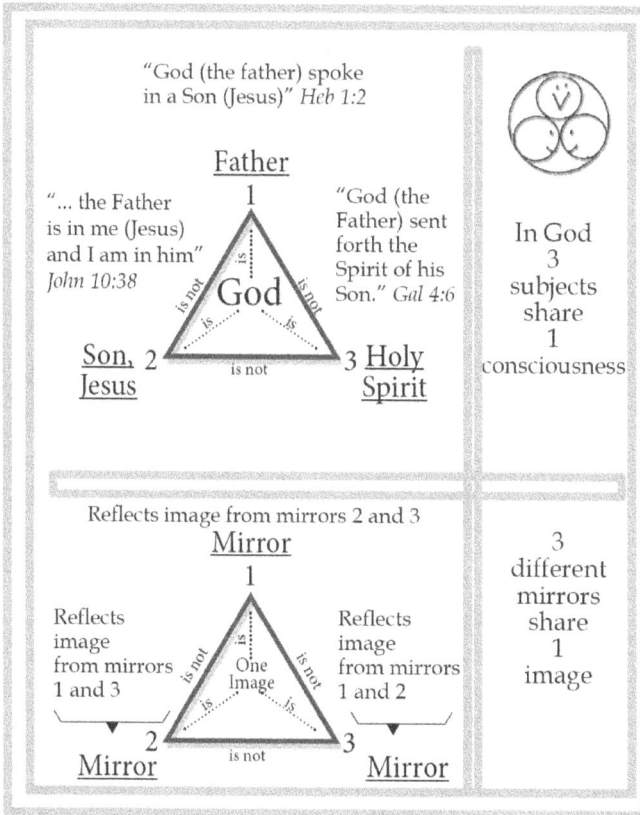

"God (the father) spoke in a Son (Jesus)" *Heb 1:2*

Father
1

"... the Father is in me (Jesus) and I am in him" *John 10:38*

"God (the Father) sent forth the Spirit of his Son." *Gal 4:6*

God
is not

is
is
is not
is not

Son, Jesus 2

is not

3 **Holy Spirit**

In God
3
subjects
share
1
consciousness

Reflects image from mirrors 2 and 3
Mirror
1

Reflects image from mirrors 1 and 3

Reflects image from mirrors 1 and 2

One Image
is
is
is not
is not

2 **Mirror**

is not

3 **Mirror**

3
different
mirrors
share
1
image

A person's word remains inside while going out to others. By analogy, the Father's Word (Jesus) remains inside the Father, though sent out into the world as Jesus.

John 1:14; 1:18

I and the Father are one.

John 10:30

Jesus does not say: "I am the Father," or that the Father and Son are one subject. The Father is in the Son since the Father and Son share one divine nature.

X. Early Christians Speak of the Trinity

The Bible reveals the triune nature of God. Together the OT and NT reveal the following three subjects: God (the Father), God's Word or Son, and the Holy Spirit. This one God of three subjects is revealed throughout the Bible. Two examples in the NT where the three are spoken of together are *Matthew 28:19 and 2 Corinthians 13:13.*

Go therefore and teach all nations, baptizing them in the name of the Father, and of the Son, and of the Holy Spirit.
Matt 28:19

In the OT the Trinity is revealed, but in a somewhat hidden manner. First, the plural word for God "Elohim" is used 2570 times. In the OT in *Genesis 1:2* and *26* this plurality is clearly revealed.

God then said: "Let <u>us</u> make man in <u>our</u>

image." - *Gen 1:26*

The word "Trinity" does not appear in the Bible; but the triune nature of God does appear throughout the Bible. This fact was taught from the beginning by the early church fathers. In this section the triune statements of several early writers will be presented.

FIRST, Clement, the fourth bishop of Rome, will be discussed. The first three bishops of Rome had been Peter, Linus, and Anencletus. Early documents indicate that St. Peter died a martyr when Nero was the emperor, probably in the year 64 AD. Linus and "Cletus" may also have died during Nero's persecution of Christians in Rome between 64-68 AD.

Clement's 25-page disciplinary letter to the Church at Corinth contains no specific date of composition. However, a number of scholars believe it was written sometime between 68-70 AD. They hold to this date because of two passages within the letter itself. The first is chapter 41: 1-2 where Clement speaks of animal sacrifices being currently offered within the Jerusalem Temple. This is important because Jerusalem and its Temple were burned to the ground in 70 AD by the Roman general Titus.

After that date Jewish religion no longer sacrificed animals in their worship. The synagogue, with its study of the Old Testament, became the normal form of Jewish worship.

Continual sacrifices are offered ... in Jerusalem ... in front of the inner Temple on the altar of sacrifice; and the [animal] offerings are first inspected for blemishes by the high priest and his ministers ...

Chapter 41: 1-2

The second reason for the early date comes from chapter 5: 1-7 in the letter. In this passage the deaths of Saint Peter and Saint Paul are said to have occurred within "our own generation."

Consider the noble examples of our own generation . . . These pillars were persecuted . . . even unto death . . . Peter . . . went to the place of glory . . .

Chapter 5: 1-7

The specific passages within Clement's letter that speak of the Trinity are found in several places: chapters 2, 12, 13, 22, 42, 46, and 58. Here are two examples.

Have we not all the same God [the Father], and the same Christ? Is not the same Spirit of grace shed upon us?

Chapter 46

As surely as God [the Father] lives, as Jesus Christ lives, and the Holy Spirit also ...

Chapter 58

Notice in this quotation that each of the three subjects in God "lives."

SECOND, Ignatius of Antioch (50?-107AD), the third bishop of Antioch, will be examined. Ignatius was arrested in Antioch for being too Christian. He was taken 1600 miles to Rome where he died in the mouths of wild animals in the Roman Colosseum. The Colosseum was built between 70-82 AD. It was a concrete structure, stadium-like, with a seating capacity of 50,000. It is still standing in Rome today. Ignatius wrote seven letters during his journey to Rome. Six of these letters were addressed to churches in six Roman cities. A seventh letter was addressed to Bishop Polycarp (69-155 AD) of Smyrna. Polycarp had probably been appointed a bishop by the Apostle John. (See Tertullians' *De Praescriptione* 32) Ignatius spoke of the Trinity in at least eight passages in four of his seven letters. Three examples will be presented.

To the church at Philadelphia: "To the church of God the Father and the Lord Jesus Christ at Philadelphia ... and confirmed ... by his Holy Spirit... That was the preaching of the Spirit, telling you never to act independently of the bishop... and to be imitators of Jesus Christ as He was of His Father."

To the Church at Smyrna: "To the Church of God the Father and our beloved Jesus Christ ... with all the gifts of the Spirit ..."

To the Church at Magnesia: "... that everything you do ...may be ...in faith and love: in the Son (Jesus) and the Father and in the (Holy) Spirit."

THIRD, Justin Martyr (c.100-165 AD) who was born into a pagan family about the time when Ignatius of Antioch died. As a young man Justin studied Greek philosophy. He eventually became a Christian and founded a Christian school in Rome. About 148 AD, Justin began writing his "Apology," a book demonstrating the rational nature of the Christian religion.

Justin Martyr wrote many passages suggesting the triune nature of God. Three examples will be given.

(1) Apology 1:10-13
"... in the name of God, the Father and Christ who was crucified under Pontius Pilate ... and the Holy Spirit, who foretold the whole story of Jesus through the (OT) prophets." Here the One Name of God includes three subjects: Father, Christ, and the Holy Spirit.

(2) Apology 61-Baptism
"They are taken to a place where there is water (for Baptism); and there they are reborn ... in the Name of God, the Father and Lord of all, and of our Savior Jesus

Christ, and of the Holy Spirit. Thus they receive the washing with water."

(3) Apology 65-66 Eucharist

"Then there is brought to the president of the brothers bread and a cup of ... wine. Taking them, he gives praise and glory to the Father of all, through the name of the Son and of the Holy Spirit ... We call this food Eucharist and no one is permitted to receive it unless he believes our teaching and has been washed for the remission of sins and for re-generation (baptized) ..."

FOURTH, Athenagoras of Athens was a Christian thinker who addressed a Christian "Plea" for understanding to the Emperor Marcus Aurelius in 177 AD. The "Plea for Christians" is a work that refutes accusations made by pagans against Christians. Within this work are several references to the Trinity.

(1) Plea 6

"God (the Father) has formed all things by his Logos (Word), and holds them in being by His Spirit." This passage says that the creation of the universe is the work of the three subjects in God: Father,

His "Logos' Christ, and the "Spirit."

(2) Plea 10
"Men who speak of God the Father and God the Son, and the Holy Spirit; and who speak of their power in union ..." This passage speaks of God "in union" — as Father, Son, and Spirit.

(3) Plea 12
"... the unity of these three: the Spirit, the Son, and the Father ..."

(4) Plea 24
"We acknowledge God (the Father), and the Son his Logos (or Word), and the Holy Spirit united in essence ..." This passage speaks of the three as "united in essence," or as having one divine nature. Thus, Christians worship one God, not three.

FIFTH, Irenaeus (140-202 AD), the second Bishop of Lyons (in France). Irenaeus had been a native of Smyrna, in modern-day Turkey, where in his youth he had been instructed by St. Polycarp, who was martyred in 155 AD. Irenaeus eventually studied in Rome and at the young age of thirty-eight, became the Bishop of Lyons. Later, about the year 190 AD, he advised Pope Victor of Rome concerning a matter in the Church at Ephesus. Irenaeus wrote five books collectively titled, "Against Heresies." The concern of these five books was that of "gnosticism," a kind of teaching based upon secret "knowledge"—false knowledge, as Irenaeus would say. Within the five books are many Trinity passages, several of which will be presented here.

Book 1:10,1

"The church ... received from the apostles ... faith in one God, the Father Almighty ... and in one Jesus Christ, the Son of God who became flesh for our salvation; and in the Holy Spirit, who announced through the OT prophets ... the birth (of Christ) from the Virgin (Mary) ..."

Book 3:9,2 and 18,3

"... the Word of God took flesh (Jesus), and was anointed by the Father with the Spirit; ... the Father anointed, the Son was anointed, and the Spirit was the unction (ointment)."

Book 4: Preface and 20,1

". . . man . . . was formed in the likeness of God (the Father) and molded by his hands, that is, by the Son and the Holy Spirit ... always present with him were the Word and Wisdom, the Son and the Spirit, by whom and in whom He made all things."

Book 4:20, 3-4

"... the Word, or Son was always with the Father ... Wisdom which is the Spirit was also with Him before creation ..."

The writers sampled here lived and wrote within the first 150 years of Christian history. They all spoke of the triune nature of God. And they were not alone. Every authentic Christian writer since that time has spoken of the Trinity. The triune mystery of God is at the heart of Christianity and of life.

"... the love of God (the Father) is poured out into our hearts through the Holy Spirit given to us (by Christ)."

Romans 5:5

About the Author

Roger Skrenes studied history and
science as an undergraduate, and
holds a master's degree in religion.
He also taught high school for
many years in Los Angeles.

His other books include:

History of the Eucharist (2017)

and

The Jesus Code (2016)

www.ingramcontent.com/pod-product-compliance
Lightning Source LLC
Chambersburg PA
CBHW022012090426
42741CB00007B/1002